T0305915

# Petrarch and Boccaccio in the First Commentaries on Dante's *Commedia*

This text proposes a reinterpretation of the history behind the canon of the *Tre Corone* (*Three Crowns*), which consists of the three great Italian authors of the fourteenth century – Dante, Petrarch and Boccaccio.

Examining the first commentaries on Dante's *Commedia*, the book argues that the elaboration of the canon of the *Tre Corone* does not date back to the fifteenth century but instead to the last quarter of the fourteenth century. The investigation moves from Guglielmo Maramauro's commentary – circa 1373, and the first exegetical text in which we can find explicit quotations from Petrarch and Boccaccio – to the major commentators of the second half of the fourteenth century: Benvenuto da Imola, Francesco da Buti and the Anonimo Fiorentino. The work focuses on the conceptual and poetic continuity between Dante, Petrarch and Boccaccio as identified by the first interpreters of the *Commedia*, demonstrating that contemporary readers and intellectuals immediately recognised a strong affinity between these three authors based on criteria not merely linguistic or rhetorical.

The findings and conclusions of this work are of great interest to scholars of Dante, as well as those studying medieval poetry and Italian literature.

**Luca Fiorentini** is Research Assistant at the University of Rome 'La Sapienza', Italy.

# Young Feltrinelli Prize in the Moral Sciences

Roberto Antonelli
*President, Class of Moral Sciences, Accademia Nazionale dei Lincei*
Alberto Quadrio Curzio
*President Emeritus, Accademia Nazionale dei Lincei*
Alessandro Roncaglia
*Joint Academic Administrator, Accademia Nazionale dei Lincei*

The Accademia Nazionale dei Lincei, founded in 1603, is one of the oldest academies in the world. Since 2018 it has assigned four "Young Antonio Feltrinelli Prizes" every two years, directed to Italian researchers in the fields of moral sciences and humanities who are less than 40 years old. Each winner is then requested to write a book-length essay on their research and/or the perspectives of research in their field, directed to the general public. The Routledge Young Feltrinelli Prize in the Moral Sciences series thus includes high-quality essays by top young researchers, providing thoroughly readable contributions to different research fields. With this initiative, Accademia dei Lincei not only gives a remarkable grant to the winners of the prize in order to support their research activity, but also contributes to the international diffusion of the research of eminent young Italian scholars.

**Business Negotiations and the Law**
The Protection of Weak Professional Parties in Standard Form Contracting
*Carlotta Rinaldo*

**Democratizing the Economics Debate**
Pluralism and Research Evaluation
*Carlo D'Ippoliti*

**Petrarch and Boccaccio in the First Commentaries on Dante's**
***Commedia***
A Literary Canon Before its Official Birth
*Luca Fiorentini*

For more information about this series, please visit: www.routledge.com/Young-Feltrinelli-Prize-in-the-Moral-Sciences/book-series/YFP

# Petrarch and Boccaccio in the First Commentaries on Dante's *Commedia*

## A Literary Canon Before its Official Birth

**Luca Fiorentini**

Routledge
Taylor & Francis Group

LONDON AND NEW YORK

First published 2020
by Routledge
2 Park Square, Milton Park, Abingdon, Oxon OX14 4RN

and by Routledge
52 Vanderbilt Avenue, New York, NY 10017

*Routledge is an imprint of the Taylor & Francis Group, an informa business*

© 2020 Luca Fiorentini

The right of Luca Fiorentini to be identified as author of this work has been
asserted by him in accordance with sections 77 and 78 of the Copyright,
Designs and Patents Act 1988.

*British Library Cataloguing-in-Publication Data*
A catalogue record for this book is available from the British Library

*Library of Congress Cataloging-in-Publication Data*
A catalog record for this book has been requested

ISBN: 978-0-367-34199-2 (hbk)
ISBN: 978-0-429-32444-4 (ebk)

Typeset in Times New Roman
by Apex CoVantage, LLC

To Elisa, Andrea, Eleonora, Damiano, Francesca,
Francesco

# Contents

# About the author

**Luca Fiorentini** (Piacenza, Italy, 1984) is Research Assistant at the University of Rome 'La Sapienza', Italy. He obtained his bachelor (2006) and master (2008) degrees in modern philology at the University of Pavia, his PhD (2012) in philology, linguistics and literature at the University of Rome 'La Sapienza'. As Post-doctoral Fellow he was enrolled at the Istituto italiano per gli studi storici in Naples (2011–13), at the Université de Paris-Sorbonne (2013–14), at the Collège de France (2014–17) and then at the University of Toronto, Department of Italian Studies (2017–2019). In 2018, he was awarded the 'Antonio Feltrinelli Giovani' Prize for Art and Poetry Criticism by the Accademia Nazionale dei Lincei. His scientific interests are mostly focused on the early critical reception of Dante Alighieri's *Commedia*. In 2016, he published his first monograph, *Per Benvenuto da Imola. Le linee ideologiche del commento dantesco* (Bologna: il Mulino, 2016). He also writes about contemporary literature for *L'Indice dei libri del mese* and *Alias Domenica-Il Manifesto*.

# Prologue

The canon constituted by the three great authors of the Italian Middle Ages – Dante, Petrarch and Boccaccio – is commonly known as the canon of the *Tre Corone* (*Three Crowns*). This name has a precise birth date: it appears for the first time in a rather bizarre work, the so-called *Paradiso degli Alberti*, written by Giovanni Gherardi in Florentine vernacular in the winter of 1425–1426.[1] In the opening pages of this work, we read:

> I ardently desire to do everything necessary – with all due apologies, of course – to exalt and ennoble my mother tongue, though it has already been exalted and ennobled by the three crowns of Florence [*tre corone fiorentine*]. I follow their model with the greatest humility, as wise sailors, in their voyages, have ever followed the pole star.[2]

The words of Giovanni Gherardi have a polemical tone; his apologies are purely rhetorical. In the years in which Gherardi wrote the passage that I have cited here, the vernacular was not universally recognised as a literary language. Indeed, many intellectuals of the fifteenth century held that to write in the vernacular necessarily meant to write for plebeian readers, bereft of culture. In the first book of the *Dialogi ad Petrum Paulum Histrum* by Leonardo Bruni (1401), Niccolò Niccoli, with evident contempt, proclaims that the masterpiece of Dante, the *Commedia*, is a work for "the wool workers, the millers and the commoners in general", and that for this reason Dante should not be considered a poet at all (§ 44).[3] But even Coluccio Salutati, who in the first book of Bruni's *Dialogi* plays the role of Niccoli's adversary, admits (§ 40): "If Dante had written in another language, I would not limit myself to setting him side by side with our ancient authors, but I would place him even above them and the Greeks".[4]

Gherardi strenuously opposes these opinions. But Gherardi's position, at the beginning of the fifteenth century, was a minority one, for a variety of reasons. There were some who despised the vernacular, as has been said.

But even those who did not despise it – as for example Leonardo Bruni, according to whom poetry in the vernacular had the same dignity as poetry in Latin[5] – did not specifically associate Dante, Petrarch and Boccaccio on account of their writings in vernacular. On the other hand, Niccolò Niccoli himself, in the first book of Bruni's *Dialogi*, turned words of censure upon Boccaccio and Petrarch as well, but not for their most famous works in the vernacular, the *Decameron* and the *Rerum vulgarium fragmenta* (or *Canzoniere*). Niccoli criticised Petrarch for the *Africa*, a poem in Latin that he judged to be of very little value. Concerning Boccaccio, Niccoli limited himself to saying that he was inferior both to Dante and to Petrarch and that for this reason he did not merit even being held in consideration. Great literature, according to Niccoli, was not that of the previous century but that of antiquity: "I prefer by far a single letter of Cicero, or a single ode by Virgil, to all the minor works of these authors of yours". And Niccoli was not the only one in those times to think in this way.

However, in the second book of the *Dialogi*, Niccoli reveals that his fierce devaluation of Dante, Petrarch and Boccaccio was entirely fictitious, and he therefore retracts it, speaking high praise of the three authors. He begins with Dante, to whom he dedicates a great deal of space (§§ 70–78). Now, Dante's vernacular is considered in a positive light: Niccoli affirms that in the tercets of the *Commedia* the highest doctrinal subjects are treated in an excellently clear and effective way, better than any professional theologian or philosopher could have managed. Even the vernacular of Petrarch receives brief praise (§ 83): Petrarch, Niccoli claims, "did not wish to abstain from popular forms of poetry, but in them, as indeed in every field, he demonstrated great elegance and eloquence".[6] So far as Boccaccio is concerned (§ 87), Niccoli makes no reference whatsoever to his vernacular work: Boccaccio is praised above all for his great encyclopedic and historical Latin works, *Genealogie Deorum Gentilium*, *De montibus*, *De casibus virorum illustrium*, *De mulieribus claris*, and so forth. In other words, Niccolò Niccoli's retraction does not imply any concession to the argument which Giovanni Gherardi would develop – namely, that Dante, Petrarch and Boccaccio excelled in the composition of vernacular literary texts.

All of this appears most curious. When we think of the canon of the *Tre Corone*, we think, essentially, of a linguistic and rhetorical canon: from the beginning of the sixteenth century and onward, Dante, Petrarch and Boccaccio were considered as the indispensable models for the elaboration of a literary 'Italian' language. At the beginning of the fifteenth century, their centrality was already recognised, but not on account of the language that they employed in those works that – as much for the readers of the sixteenth century as for us – were regarded as their masterpieces: the *Commedia*, the *Canzoniere* and the *Decameron*. The words of Giovanni Gherardi, considered in their historical and cultural context, are therefore not only rare but even quite unusual and original: at the beginning of the fifteenth century, Gherardi was essentially the only person to consider Dante, Petrarch and Boccaccio as the 'three crowns' of the vernacular. But how to explain all of this? If Dante, Petrarch and Boccaccio are not united by the fact that all of them wrote their most important works in their mother tongue, on the basis of what elements – and what works – did the readers of the fifteenth century hold that the three Florentine writers formed a cohesive group?

Let us take a step back. We owe the first explicit formalisation of this canon of vernacular literature, constituted by Dante, Petrarch and Boccaccio, to Petrarch himself – but his is a decidedly ambiguous formalisation. In his letter *Sen.* V.2, which he sent to Boccaccio in 1365, Petrarch seeks to console his friend, who thought himself so inferior in the writing of vernacular verses that he had decided to burn his own compositions. Petrarch writes as follows (§§ 30–34):

> Take care lest it really be pride that you cannot endure second or third place, or that I should surpass you when I wish to be your equal, or that the master of our vernacular literature should be preferred to you. Do you bear it so ill to be thus outdone by one or two men, especially fellow citizens, or at most very few? Take care lest this be more conceited than coveting first place. To aspire to the highest can be viewed as magnanimity; to scorn what is next to highest somehow seems like conceit. I understand that the old gentleman from Ravenna, a competent judge of such matters, always likes to assign you third place whenever the subject comes up. If this is too lowly, I appear to block your way to first place, which I do not do, look, I gladly yield and leave second place to you.[7]

I limit myself to highlighting two elements here: granting the truth of Petrarch's words, an "old gentleman from Ravenna" was the first to recognise the absolute superiority of Dante ("the master of our vernacular literature"), of Boccaccio and of Petrarch himself in vernacular poetry, thus reuniting their names under the same sign. Who was this man? In all probability Petrarch refers here to Menghino Mezzani, a notary of Ravenna born at the end of the thirteenth century, who entered into close confidence with Dante.[8] The story of the *Tre Corone* – as Giovanni Gherardi conceives it – begins therefore at a very early date, even ten years before the death of two members of the triad, Petrarch and Boccaccio. But there is a problem – and here we come to the second point. The problem is that Petrarch does not wish to be a part of this canon. In the passage that I have transcribed, Petrarch declares that he would be happy to leave the second place to Boccaccio: "I gladly yield and leave second place to you". A bit further on, he explains why (§§ 52–55):

> I had . . . the . . . idea to devote all my time to vernacular pursuits since the loftier Latin style – both prose and poetry – had been so highly polished by ancient talents that now my resources, or anyone else's, can add very little. On the other hand, this vernacular writing, just invented, still new, showed itself capable of great improvement and development after having been ravaged by many and cultivated by very few husbandmen. Well then, this hope so attracted me and at the same time the spur of youth so urged me onward that I undertook a great work in that style; and having laid, as it were, the foundations of that edifice, I gathered the cement and stone and wood; I then began to observe attentively our age, mother of pride and laziness, and to notice the great talent of the show-offs, the charm of their elocution, so that you would say the words were not being recited but torn to pieces; hearing this once, twice, many more times, and repeating it to myself more and more, I finally came to realize that it was a waste of effort to build on soft mud and shifting sand, and that I and my work would be torn to shreds by the hands of the mob.

Petrarch does not want to be remembered for his vernacular works. These are, in fact, the fruit of a still precocious phase of his poetic career. In his youth, Petrarch had let himself be taken in by a language which was essentially devoid of tradition, and thus open to improvement. But he had quickly changed his mind: "it was a waste of effort to build on soft mud and shifting sand". The vernacular is compared to unstable and uncertain materials: by its nature, it is indeed an irremediably mutable language. The proof is furnished by those uncultivated readers who destroy ("[tear] to pieces") the verses of the vernacular poets by repeating them badly. This occurs in an entirely natural way, since the vernacular is a language devoid of rules: anyone at all may take it up and modify it at will. For this reason, Petrarch declares that he has definitively determined to follow "another pathway", the "straighter and higher" ("rectius atque altius") path of writing in the immutable language of the classics, Latin.

As can be intuited, this is a passage of some decisive importance, and it explains many things. Above all, we find here an argument used also by Niccolò Niccoli in the first book of his *Dialogi ad Petrum Paulum Histrum*: the (wilfully exaggerated) idea that the beneficiaries of vernacular works are popular readers. As we have seen, Niccoli employs this argument against Dante, and Petrarch did the same in another important epistle sent to

Boccaccio some years before the *Sen.* V.2: namely, the *Fam.* XXI.15, which I will cite frequently in the coming chapters. But there is more: Petrarch asks to be considered as a Latin poet, not as a vernacular poet. On the one hand, this explains the tendency in the authors whom I have cited to keep silent about Petrarch's vernacular production. On the other hand, it demonstrates that, from its very origins, the canon which would later be named the *Tre Corone* presented itself as an intrinsically conflictual canon.

Many consequences follow from this, and they concern, in the first place, the earliest reception of Dante. Petrarch, as many humanists of the subsequent century, had indeed harshly criticised Dante for having written his most important work in a language unworthy of the enthusiasts of high poetry. In the *Fam.* XXI.15 Petrarch returns to this point obsessively. And he does so also to criticise the other member of the triad, Boccaccio, who in his carmen *Ytalie iam certus honos* (1351–1353) attempted to convince him of the goodness of Dante's linguistic choices (vv. 2–6): "welcome this work of Dante, which is appreciated by the learned and loved also by the people, and written in a style that in my judgement has no equal, not even in previous centuries. Do not be displeased when you read the verses of this exiled poet, that they be written in his mother tongue".[9] In his writings on the *Commedia*, Boccaccio cannot help but confront the negative judgement that Petrarch had passed on the vernacular: and the consequences of this for the general interpretation of Dante will not be insignificant, as we will see in detail in the first chapter of this book.

But Boccaccio was not the only of the early Dante commentators to have to come to terms with the Petrarchian devaluation of Dante's language.[10] Petrarch's name begins to appear very early in the commentaries on the *Commedia*, starting already from the end of the 1360s, and it is immediately associated with the name of Boccaccio. An interpreter from Naples, Guglielmo Maramauro, would become the first to cite the names of Petrarch and Boccaccio in his commentary on Dante's *Inferno*, composed between 1369 and 1373. Maramauro goes so far as to write that Petrarch and Boccaccio have helped him to interpret Dante: "I began this difficult task [i.e. the commentary on Dante's *Commedia*] with the help of Messer Giovanni Boccaccio and Messer Francesco Petrarca".[11] I will return to these surprising words in the second chapter of this book, where I will attentively examine them.

A few years after Maramauro, between 1375 and 1383, another interpreter of Dante's *Commedia* demonstrates his full awareness of the role that Dante, Petrarch and Boccaccio had assumed in the panorama of modern literature; moreover, he reflects on the motives for which these men might be considered the greatest poets of their times. The name of this commentator is Benvenuto da Imola, and I will dedicate the greater part of this book to him (Chapters 3 and 4). Benvenuto is familiar with a large number of works by Boccaccio and Petrarch, as we will have occasion to see. Significantly, he never (or almost never) cites Petrarch's vernacular texts. The commentators who come after Benvenuto also much prefer the Latin Petrarch to the Vernacular Petrarch. The so-called Anonimo Fiorentino (the 'Anonymous Florentine'), whose commentary on the *Commedia* was written between the end of the fourteenth and the beginning of the fifteenth centuries, is the only commentator of this period to cite the vernacular rhymes of Petrarch with any frequency, as we shall see (Chapter 2); but in the commentary of the Anonimo Fiorentino there are more than twice as many citations of the Latin work of Petrarch than of the vernacular work.[12] Evidently, the request formulated by Petrarch in the *Sen.* V.2 had been granted him: Dante interpreters, starting from the end of the fourteenth century, considered Petrarch above all a poet in Latin.

Bearing all of this in mind, and consequently setting aside the linguistic element, what was the element of continuity that the early commentators of the *Commedia* perceived standing between Dante, Petrarch and Boccaccio? And in what way did the reflections of Dante commentators at the end of the fourteenth century anticipate the debate on the *Tre Corone* that was to develop in the next century?

I will attempt to respond to these questions in the following pages. Naturally, this study is bound by the norms of the publisher that has so generously agreed to publish it; and since these limits in no way permit exhaustive research on the presence of Petrarch and Boccaccio in the first commentaries on Dante's *Commedia*, I propose rather to paint a partial portrait of the question, integrating the few studies which already exist on it so as to formulate some early interpretive hypotheses in response. But I will certainly dedicate myself to a deeper examination of this theme in my next works.

The canon composed of Dante, Petrarch and Boccaccio is a creation which owes its existence in the first place to Petrarch and Boccaccio themselves. But its history commences when it separates from those who created it and begins to lead an autonomous life. I maintain that this happened somewhat earlier than is generally believed,[13] and in ways that are still partially obscure. I hope that the pages which follow might contribute to shedding some initial light on this darkness.

This book would not exist, had the Accademia Nazionale dei Lincei not awarded me with the 'Antonio Feltrinelli Giovani' Prize for Art and Poetry Criticism on 9 November 2018. My gratitude toward the Accademia dei Lincei is inseparable from my sense of responsibility for the trust which has thereby been placed in me. While writing this book, I have been able to count on the generous help and the invaluable advice of Elisa Brilli, Corrado Calenda, Teresa Diluiso, Paolo Falzone, Enrico Fenzi, Sonia Gentili, Lorenzo Geri, Manuele Gragnolati, Irene Gualdo, Giorgio Inglese, Eleonora Lima, Alice Martignoni, Carlotta Mazzoncini, Andrea Mazzucchi, Carlo Ossola, Diego Parisi, Stefano Pezzé, Luca Carlo Rossi, Gennaro Sasso and Alessia Valenti. For his essential support, I express my profound gratitude to John Bruce Leonard.

## Notes

1 See H. Baron, *The Crisis of the Early Italian Renaissance: Civic Humanism and Republican Liberty in an Age of Classicism and Tyranny*, 2 vols. (Princeton, NJ: Princeton University Press, 1955), vol. 1, 297–299, and S. Gilson, *Dante and Renaissance Florence* (Cambridge: Cambridge University Press, 2005), 76–77.
2 The translation is mine. See Giovanni Gherardi da Prato, *Il Paradiso degli Alberti*, ed. by A. Lanza (Rome: Salerno, 1975), 3–4.
3 Here and in what follows, all translations of Bruni's *Dialogi* are mine. For the original text, see L. Bruni, *Dialogi ad Petrum Paulum Histrum*, ed. by S. U. Baldassarri (Florence: Olschki, 1994), 255–256. On the reception of Dante' oeuvre during the Renaissance, see the fundamental monographs by Gilson, *Dante and Renaissance Florence*, and *Reading Dante in Renaissance Italy: Florence, Venice and the Divine Poet* (Cambridge: Cambridge University Press, 2018).
4 Bruni, *Dialogi*, 253.
5 Translation mine. See L. Bruni, *Le vite di Dante e del Petrarca*, ed. by M. Berté and R. Rognoni, in *Le vite di Dante dal XIV al XVI secolo*, ed. by M. Berté, M. Fiorilla, S. Chiodo and I. Valente (Rome: Salerno, 2017), 243.
6 See Bruni, *Dialogi*, 258, 265–269 and 271.
7 I quote, here and in the next paragraph, the translation of A. S. Bernardo, S. Levin and R. A. Bernardo: see F. Petrarch, *Letters of Old Age: Rerum senilium libri I–XVIII*, vol. 1, *Books I–IX* (Baltimore-London: The Johns Hopkins University Press, 1992), 157–166. I will cite this letter again in the first chapter of this book.
8 The first to identify the "old gentleman from Ravenna" with Menghino Mezzani was C. Ricci, *L'ultimo rifugio di Dante* (1921), new edition by E. Chiarini (Ravenna: Longo, 1965), 203. See also F. Petrarca, *Senile V 2*, ed. by M. Berté (Florence: Le Lettere, 1998), 15–16.
9 Translation mine. I quote from G. Boccaccio, *Tutte le opere*, vol. V/1, ed. by V. Branca *et alii* (Milan: Mondadori, 1992), 430. I will discuss this work at further length in the first chapter of this book. See, for now, M. Eisner, *Boccaccio and the Invention of Italian Literature* (Cambridge: Cambridge University Press, 2013), 12–16.
10 For a review of all the first commentaries on the *Commedia*, see S. Bellomo, 'Introduzione', in *Dizionario dei commentatori danteschi* (Florence: Olschki, 2004), 1–49, Z. G. Barański, 'L'esegesi medievale della *Commedia* e il problema delle fonti', in *"Chiosar con altro testo". Leggere Dante nel Trecento* (Florence: Cadmo, 2001), 13–39, and A. Mazzucchi, 'Nota introduttiva', in *Censimento dei commenti danteschi*, ed. by E. Malato and A. Mazzucchi, vol. 1,

*I commenti di tradizione manoscritta (fino al 1428)* (Rome: Salerno, 2011), tome 1 XXI–XXXIII.

11  G. Maramauro, *Expositione sopra l' "Inferno"*, ed. by S. Bellomo (Padua: Antenore Editrice, 1998), 82.

12  See F. Geymonat, 'Fonti non esegetiche nel commento alla *Commedia* dell'Anonimo Fiorentino', *Rivista di studi danteschi* 2 (2002), 359–377.

13  See for example G. Alfano, 'Tra Dante e Petrarca: Boccaccio e l'invenzione della tradizione (ancora sulla politica degli autori)', in *Boccaccio: gli antichi e i moderni*, ed. by A. M. Cabrini and A. D'Agostino (Milan: Ledizioni, 2018), 93.

# 1 Poetry, language, allegory
## Dante in the hands of Petrarch and Boccaccio

### Legends and conflicts: a (mysterious) background narrative

We can begin with a tale, or rather with a legend – or better yet, with a very peculiar origin myth. Around the beginning of the '40s of the fourteenth century, Giovanni Boccaccio transcribed in his 'Zibaldone Laurenziano' an enigmatic and fascinating epistle for which there exists no other direct evidence.[1] For more than four centuries this text remained completely unknown. Some of the sensational reports contained within it were brought to light only thanks to Boccaccio himself: as we will see, Boccaccio related these reports in some of the most important essays which he dedicated to Dante's work, the *Trattatello in laude di Dante* (first draft, §§ 192–193; second draft, §§ 128–131) and the *Esposizioni sopra la "Comedia"* (*accessus*, §§ 75–77), without ever mentioning, however, the source from which he had taken them. The first person to make this document accessible in modern times was the erudite Lorenzo Mehus, who, in 1759, printed it in the preface to his edition of the Latin letters of Ambrogio Traversari. Prior to that date, nobody, excluding of course Boccaccio, had any way of knowing of it directly.[2]

Let us examine this mysterious text. As already mentioned, it is a letter; the sender appears to be a Benedictine friar of the Santa Croce del Corvo Monastery in Lunigiana: his name is Ilaro. All of this is declared in the first paragraph of the letter, the *salutatio*:

> To the renowned and magnificent lord Uguccione della Faggiuola, highly pre-eminent amongst Italian magnates, Brother Ilaro, a humble monk of Corvo, at the mouth of the Macra wishes salvation in Him who is the true salvation of us all.[3]

Ilaro wrote to the *podestà* of Pisa, Uguccione della Faggiuola, in order to send to him a manuscript received from a mysterious man, a traveller who had arrived some time before in his monastery. The letter offers no explicit indications about the date of the meeting between Ilaro and this man, but the implicit chronological references permit us to formulate at least a hypothesis: Uguccione, indicated as "renowned and magnificent lord", took possession of Pisa on 20 September 1313 and of Lucca on 14 June 1314; Moroello Malaspina, mentioned in the last paragraph of the letter as still living (§ 14), died on 18 April 1315. The episode narrated in the letter should therefore be placed in a period of time delineated by these dates, from the end of 1313 – or rather the whole of 1314 – to the beginning of 1315. It was precisely in this window of time, it would seem, that Dante's *Inferno* enjoyed its first diffusion.[4]

But let us take up once more the thread of our story. The name of the traveller is never revealed in the letter, but, continuing to read this text – which, as we shall see, contains a considerable series of exceptional revelations – we understand that it was Dante. Though Ilaro lived in a context of substantial isolation, he claims to have received news of Dante's fame long before knowing him personally. The friar writes in fact that he knew that this man, from an early age, had been skilled at expressing "in vernacular speech", and in poetry, concepts that the greatest classical authors would barely have been able to express in Latin (§§ 4–5):

> as I have learnt from others – and very wonderful it is – before he had passed from childhood he attempted to utter unheard-of things, and – this is wonderful yet – he strove to express what in vernacular speech can scarcely be expressed in Latin itself by the most eminent authors. And I do not mean in straightforward vernacular, but in that of a song.

What follows is decidedly surprising – and curious, and valuable from the literary point of view. Dante introduced himself, and thus Ilaro learned that the man standing before him was the poet whose fame he had long known: "For though I had never once seen him before that day, his fame had long before reached me". Dante appreciated the friar's interest and decided to return his attention with a sign of affection, such as presupposed a great deal of trust. He handed him a manuscript containing a text that before then had been certainly unknown to him: "'Here', he said, 'is a part of my work, which I take it you have never seen'" (§ 8). Reading the last paragraph of the letter (§ 14), we understand that the text which Dante gave to Ilaro was none other than the *Inferno*.

Ilaro therefore found himself holding the initial *cantica* of the *Commedia* in his hands. And there is no doubt that, based on this tale, he was one of its first readers – perhaps even the very first. What is the reaction of the Benedictine friar to Dante's masterpiece? It is certainly an unpredictable reaction, from our point of view. First, gratitude, emotion and lively curiosity – and this, naturally, does not make us wonder. Then, however, follows something we would not expect. Let us read what Ilaro writes (§ 9):

> I took it joyfully to my bosom, opened it, and in his presence fixed my eyes intently upon it. And when I observed that the words were vernacular, and manifested some kind of wonder, he asked me what I was boggling at. And I answered that I was astonished at the quality of the language, partly because I thought it seemed difficult, no, inconceivable, that such arduous matter could have been expressed in the vernacular, and partly because it seemed incongruous for so much learning to be combined with a plebeian garb.

All of this, it is needless to say it, is highly implausible. The idea that the immediate reaction of one of the first readers of the *Commedia* should be disappointment at the language used by Dante is unrealistic, and almost even comes across as forced; for this reason, it is quite indicative of the thought that animated the author of this document – which is to say, the inventor of this story. I should indeed clarify at this point that Ilaro's letter is not an authentic document; it has the semblance of one, but the reports that it contains are surely false, at least for the most part. This does not mean, however, that the letter is necessarily the work of an individual acting with the intent of creating a counterfeit document so as to profit thereby. If we examine the document as a whole, Ilaro's letter seems in fact to be, "rather than a malicious 'forgery', . . . a school exercise of good quality, on the theme 'Dante replies to the humanistic objections regarding the language of the poem'".[5]

As has been observed, Ilaro's reaction to Dante's *Inferno* implies a harshly negative judgement on the vernacular. And this judgement is, moreover, explicit: Ilaro defines the vernacular as *amiculum populare*, namely 'plebeian garment', using a metaphor that serves precisely to indicate a means of expression typical of the uncultured. With this definition of the vernacular, Ilaro demonstrates that he is perfectly in accord with the linguistic thought of early humanism, which was almost always hostile to those forms of literary creations that do not employ Latin, the language of the classics.

How does Dante react to Ilaro's critique? Surprisingly, he takes it quite well: he is not irritated and even recognises a degree of legitimacy in his interlocutor's arguments. But he does not fail to defend himself, and in so doing he makes a remarkable proclamation (§§ 10–11):

> To this, he answered: "Certainly you have reason in your thoughts; and when first the seed, maybe implanted by Heaven, began to sprout towards such a purpose, I chose the language rightly belonging to the

same, and not only chose but (versifying in it after the accustomed fashion) I began:

> Ultima rengna canam fluvido contermina mundo,
> Spiritibus que lata patent, que premia solvunt,
> Pro meritis cuicunque suis.[6]

But when I pondered on the conditions of the present age, I saw how the works of the great poets are flung aside almost as things of nothing. And so men of high birth, for whom such works were written in a better age have – shame on them! – abandoned the liberal arts to the common folk. And so I put aside the lyre to which I had trusted, and tuned another, in harmony with the tastes of the moderns; for in vain is tooth-food put to the mouths of them that suck".

This passage deserves to be carefully examined. Dante recounts that when he first had the inspiration that would lead him to compose the *Commedia*, he did not have any doubt about the fact that he would obey that inspiration by writing in Latin. Indeed, that is how he began: and as proof of this, he recites aloud to Ilaro, who promptly wrote them down, the first two and a half hexameters of this original and otherwise unknown Latin draft of the poem. This is, as already said, remarkable. And it is in fact on account of this report that Ilaro's letter has enjoyed a certain degree of fortune among the academics and has been the subject, even up to recent times, of various debates regarding its authenticity.

The project of writing the *Commedia* in Latin was however interrupted almost immediately; the reason for this choice is explained in the second part of the passage. Dante realised very quickly that the ideal addressees of the *Commedia*, the men of high rank ("generosi homines"), would not be able to understand a text written in any language other than the 'common' one, as they no longer had any great familiarity with Latin, the language of the classics. The poetry and the other liberal arts, Dante admits bitterly, have by now in fact become the dominion of the uncultured ("liberales artes, pro dolor, dimisere plebeis").

At this point arises another very curious fact, which, however, so far as I know, has roused less interest among scholars. Dante stops talking and makes a gesture, accompanying it with an expression of affection. He hands the manuscript of his work to Ilaro and asks him – this is the surprising particularity – to produce a commentary on it (§ 12):

> And after saying this, he added, with much affection, that if I could have leisure for such occupations, I was to go through the work with certain brief annotations, and send it on, so annotated, to you.

The unlikelihood of the events narrated in the letter here touches its apogee. Not only did Dante supposedly commission a friar, whom he met by mere chance upon the road, to deliver the *Inferno* to Uguccione della Faggiuola, but he also asks the same friar to write a commentary upon it. I have already said that it is likely that Ilaro's letter is not the work of a man acting with the aim of circulating false reports, but that it is probably rather a scholarly exercise, composed by no one knows whom and fallen no one knows how into Boccaccio's hands. In any case, the implausibility of this detail – that Dante bids a friar he has only just met to write a commentary on his *Inferno* – demands explanation: it is in fact too unrealistic an invention to believe that it is not the product of some design. In addition, the reference to Ilaro's commentary is reiterated on several occasions throughout the letter: not only in the passage that we have just read but already from the beginning (§ 4), and again at the end (§ 13), in a passage to which I will return shortly. The entire letter, in other words, is presented as if it were the preface of an annotated edition of the *Inferno* – as if it were the text accompanying the first commentary on Dante ever written.[7] Let us try to understand what reason the document's author might have had for imaging that Dante asks Ilaro to annotate his poem. There is in fact no doubt that this detail interests Ilaro's inventor a great deal: he repeats it many times, and insists upon it, despite its evident implausibility.

Perhaps the fact that Dante recites to Ilaro the original Latin *incipit* of the *Commedia* – and that Ilaro promptly transcribes it, sparing it in this way from oblivion – serves not only to confirm this report but also to eradicate a potential doubt, namely that Dante wrote in the vernacular because he was incapable of writing in Latin. That such a doubt was circulating is effectively confirmed by Boccaccio, who in vv. 8–12 of the poem *Ytalie iam certus honos* (1351–1353) wrote: "[Dante] wanted to show posterity what modern vernacular poetry was capable of doing, and his reason was certainly not – as his enemies, driven by envy, love to claim – his ignorance [of the Latin]".[8] Some time after, in the famous *Fam.* XXI.15 addressed directly to Boccaccio (1359), Petrarch would moreover express a very negative judgement on Dante's Latin production, both in prose and in poetry (§ 24): "I have at times said only one thing to those who wished to know my exact thoughts: his style was unequal, for he rises to nobler and loftier heights in the vernacular than in Latin poetry or prose".[9] Leonardo Bruni would later pass a similar judgement. In his *Life of Dante* (1436), he writes (§ 54): "Dante has certainly written very well in the vernacular that which he would not have been able to write in Latin, using the ancient metrical forms: the proof of this can be found in his *Eclogues* in hexameters, which are beautiful but do not rival those written by other poets".[10] In contrast to Petrarch, however, Bruni adds a clarification here: "Dante knew that he was much more gifted in vernacular writing and in rhyme than in Latin writing and in the ancient metrical forms" (§ 53).[11]

Where does he derive this information? We do not know. However, we can compare it to what had been written about thirty years prior by another Florentine humanist: namely, Filippo Villani, the author of an important historical work on Florence (*Liber de origine civitatis Florentie et de eiusdem famosis civibus*, 1381–1396) and of a commentary in Latin on the first canto of the *Inferno*, preceded by a long general introduction to the entire poem (1391–1405).[12] In this introduction, Villani cites the episode contained in Ilaro's letter, taking it, in all probability, from Boccaccio's *Esposizioni sopra la "Comedia"*.[13] After having reported the first two and a half hexameters of the legendary first Latin draft of the *Commedia*, and after having explained that Dante chose to continue in the vernacular so as to reach an audience which was ignorant of Latin, Villani adds:

> My uncle, the historiographer Giovanni Villani, who was a friend and political companion of Dante, once told me that Dante himself had confessed to him that, after having compared his own Latin verses with those of Virgil, Statius, Horace, Ovid and Lucan, he felt as though he had set sackcloth beside the purple, and it seemed to him that his verses could not hold up in the contest with those of the classic authors. Knowing on the other hand that he was unsurpassed in the writing of verse in the vernacular, he decided to dedicate his talent to these.[14]

According to Filippo Villani, Dante interrupted the writing of the *Commedia* in Latin hexameters not merely for 'political' reasons but also because he was aware that he was not capable of continuing. It is unlikely that this story really comes from Giovanni Villani, Filippo's uncle and the author of a famous *History* (*Cronica*) of Florence: given the large difference in age between Giovanni Villani and Dante, it is not credible that there might have been so close a relationship between the two.[15] It is probable instead that Filippo Villani uses the 'mask' of his uncle Giovanni to give voice to his own personal opinion. And it is noteworthy that this opinion is put into explicit relation with the tale of Ilaro: Villani seems indeed to insinuate that the 'positive' reasons behind Dante's linguistic choice are not the only ones – or, worse still, that they are not wholly sincere.[16] Some twenty years before Filippo Villani, another Dante commentator who knew, through Boccaccio, the legend of the original Latin draft of the *Commedia* had voiced a doubt similar to that expressed by Villani. This was Benvenuto da Imola, who, however, as we will see in the third chapter of this book, decisively rejected the possibility that Dante considered himself incapable of writing a poem in Latin hexameters. Benvenuto, too, cited a 'witness' in support of his thesis, and this time not just any witness, but rather the very last witness that anyone might expect: Petrarch. But I will come back to this surprising episode in due time.

## The representative strategy of the *Commedia* according to friar Ilaro

In point of fact, the tale of Ilaro – Dante's decision to interrupt the writing of the *Commedia* in Latin – could easily have raised suspicions similar to those expressed by Filippo Villani. It is very likely, however, that the author of Ilaro's letter had no doubts whatever on this score: indeed, his tale serves as effective witness of the contrary proposition, as we have already noted – namely, of Dante's full mastery of poetic writing in Latin. But probably there is still more here. Upon first reading the initial lines of the *Inferno*, Ilaro highlights one element in particular: that the vernacular seems an inappropriate language to express such lofty content. This means that the lowering to which Dante deliberately forced his writing concerns only the language, not the contents. The latter remains high and difficult, as Ilaro repeats at least twice: "such arduous matter", "so much learning" (§ 9).

At this point, we seem to perceive something further. Perhaps the most openly unrealistic particular of the tale – the fact that Dante considers it so important that his work be flanked by commentary that he entrusts to Ilaro himself the duty of writing it – serves precisely to reaffirm that the contents of the *Commedia* are much too high and complex for just anybody to understand them. After all, it is one thing to superficially understand a text; it is quite another to penetrate deep into its meaning. In this regard, the letter seems to offer us another intriguing detail. In the last lines of the text, Ilaro gives us a glimpse of a succinct but most interesting indication about the 'quality' of his work as interpreter. Ilaro affirms that he has drafted the annotations requested by Dante ("Quod quidem [feci]"), and then adds (§ 13):

> At this, though I have not fully extracted all that lies concealed in his words, I have faithfully and with free heart laboured. . . . And if in this anything shall seem doubtful, impute it only to my incapacity, for without doubt the text itself must need be regarded as without defects in every way.

The point that interests us is in the first phrase of this extract. The first interpreter of the *Commedia*, one moreover who benefited from direct contact with the author, Ilaro set himself to reveal the *hidden* meanings in Dante's verses. The exegesis of the *Commedia* is conceived, in other words, as an essentially allegorical exegesis.

It seems that the great problem broached at the heart of the letter ("I was astonished at the quality of the language") issues here in a partially positive solution: the search for greater linguistic accessibility was not a vehicle for conceptual simplification. Indeed, the contrary is true: not only are the contents of the *Commedia* difficult and lofty, but they are also "concealed", and therefore they were conceived only for those who have the capacity, even before understanding them, to discern them underneath the literal sense. A sort of compensating strategy seems indeed to be delineated here, if in merest sketch. If the language used by Dante is that of the uncultured, this does not imply that cultured readers can find no 'tooth-food for their mouths' in the *Commedia* (to borrow the metaphor used in § 11 of the letter). The concession made to the uncultured through the adoption of the vernacular language did not reduce the *Commedia* to a popular work, such as might be easily accessible to everybody in its entirety. Ilaro's commentary serves precisely to corroborate this. And that some commentary should be necessary is demonstrated by the fact that Dante himself asks the friar to reveal to the readers "all that lies concealed in his words".

At the beginning of this chapter, I defined the tale contained in Ilaro's letter as a legend, but also as an origin myth. Indeed, whoever invented this story also imagined that the long tradition of commentary on the *Commedia* began in this way, starting from an explicit request on the part of Dante himself. This fiction, as already said, presupposed a very clear idea of Dante's poetry, popular in style but elevated and even 'sectarian', because allegoric, in contents. And that this is the correct way to interpret the *Commedia* is confirmed, in Ilaro's narration, precisely by the fact that Dante himself declared Ilaro to be his first interpreter.

As has already been said, Boccaccio copied Ilaro's letter at the beginning of the '40s of the fourteenth century, about twenty years after Dante's death. We are therefore still in a precocious phase of the *Commedia*'s initial reception. And it is significant that this ancient document, with the mysterious and fascinating story that it transmits, appears to already serve an openly apologetic function. Whoever wrote it, and whatever his immediate goal was (To perform a simple exercise? To intentionally spread false reports?), he certainly wanted to defend Dante from those who criticised him for having written the *Commedia* in his mother tongue.

We know that even the real Dante had to answer a similar critique. At some unspecified point during Dante's residence in Ravenna, probably in the first months of 1320,[17] the Bolognese humanist Giovanni del Virgilio wrote a Latin poem to the author of the *Commedia*, in which, among other things, he asks him (*Ecl.*16–17): "such weighty themes why wilt thou still cast to the vernacular, | while we pale students shall read nought from thee as bard?"[18] Like Ilaro, Giovanni also expresses an open hostility toward the vernacular, the language spoken "at street corners by some buffoon" (*Ecl.* I.13–14). In Ilaro's judgement, the vernacular is before anything a language incongruent with the themes covered by the *Commedia*: themes so elevated would indeed require a language equally elevated, namely classical Latin. For Giovanni del Virgilio, too, Dante's vernacular is a 'base' language, which little accords with the themes treated in the poem. But Giovanni also explains *why* the vernacular cannot be considered a high language, well suited to transmitting elevated and 'universal' contents. The vernacular, writes Giovanni, is in fact an intrinsically changeable language (*Ecl.* I.15–16): "Clerks scorn the vernaculars, | even though they varied not, whereas there are a thousand idioms". To the intrinsic mutability of the vernacular languages is opposed the limpid fixedness of Latin. The language of the cultured is, in other words, the language of stability; the language of the people is that of instability, of mutability.

The dialectic between these two large notions – variety and immutability, where the first constitute a non-value and the second a supreme value – is an element of primary importance, to which we will return on several occasions and from various perspectives. It is indeed around this dialectic that the role of Boccaccio and Petrarch is defined in the first critical reception of Dante's *Commedia*: both would call each other back to it frequently, either to defend Dante's poetry or to attack it, demeaning it. And as we will see, those early commentators of Dante most exposed to the influence of Petrarch and Boccaccio would do the same.

Let us return to the question of the instability of the vernacular. Dante too, like Giovanni del Virgilio, was entirely aware that the vernacular, as opposed to Latin, is a mutable language. In fact, in the first book of the *Convivio* (chapter 5, § 7), we read: "Latin is eternal and incorruptible, while the vernacular is unstable and corruptible".[19] Precisely for this reason, Dante declares that he considers Latin – which is for him an artificial language, created to compensate for the variety of natural languages – nobler than the vernacular (I.v, §§ 7–14). Despite this, he chooses to write the *Convivio* in the vernacular. Let us recall that the *Convivio* is a philosophical treatise (which Dante wrote between 1304 and 1306 without, however, finishing it) structured in the form of a commentary on poetic texts (*canzoni*) composed by Dante himself. In the first book, Dante asks if it would be better to write this work in Latin or in the vernacular: and his choice falls resolutely on the vernacular. There are various reasons for this, but among them is the principle connected to the aim of writing a philosophical text that is comprehensible to all, both "the learned and the unlearned" (I.vii, §§ 11–12).

Ilaro's letter seems to echo this passage, disclosing it however in negative terms.[20] The (real) Dante of the *Convivio* chooses the vernacular to reach a wider public; that is, he writes his treatise toward the end of offering philosophical notions even to those who, through no fault of their own, have not had the possibility to access those places and those texts wherein philosophy is "truly revealed" (II.xii, § 7).[21] Ilaro's Dante, on the other hand, is constrained, despite himself, to adapt his work to the decadence of his times: he would like to write in Latin but must renounce it because his ideal readers would not understand it. It must be observed that even the true Dante poses the problem of how to save the vernacular from the dominion of instability and corruptibility. In his *De vulgari eloquentia*, begun in the same years as the *Convivio* (and in its turn never completed), Dante seeks to define the fundamental characteristics of an "illustrious vernacular"[22] which approaches as much as possible the stability of Latin. But the *Commedia* is not written according to the rules of the *De vulgari eloquentia*: indeed, in the *Commedia* the rules of the *De vulgari eloquentia* are constantly transgressed. Dante's vernacular in the *Commedia* is characterised by a very marked variety of languages and styles, and for this reason it is certainly comparable, as Auerbach already noted, to the great model of the *sermo humilis* of the Bible.[23]

In light of this, how did Dante reply to the accusations of Giovanni del Virgilio? The response of the real Dante has nothing to do with that of Ilaro's Dante. The real Dante does not mention the fact that his writing is allegorical nor admit to having privileged the vernacular because he was forced to do so by the cultural decadence of his epoch. And above all he declares without hesitation that if ever he should be crowned a poet, this will happen certainly thanks to the *Commedia* – and no disrespect to his interlocutor (*Ecl*. II.48–51).

The poetical exchange between Giovanni del Virgilio and Dante is strongly implied in Ilaro's letter. Not only are exactly the same questions evoked, but the two and a half hexameters of the first partial Latin draft of the *Commedia* reported in the letter of the friar are revealed, to a careful eye, as a cento of the first two texts of the correspondence between Giovanni del Virgilio and Dante. Since the exchange between Giovanni and Dante dates back certainly to a later epoch than 1314–1315 – namely, to that period in which, based on what is narrated in the letter, the meeting took place between Dante and Ilaro – we can infer that "Ilaro's letter is not authentic".[24]

What is most important here, however, is the 'cultural' testimony offered by Ilaro's letter. It permits us to ascertain that, already from the earliest reception of the *Commedia*, Dante's commentators were obliged to contest a radical critique – to wit, that Dante's vernacular was a means of expression unworthy of a cultured public.

## Boccaccio and the anti-Dantism of Petrarch

It is well known who Dante's principal detractor was, against whom Giovanni Boccaccio for several decades had to measure himself: I am referring to Petrarch. And it is equally well known that among the various strategies that Boccaccio elaborated to adapt the *Commedia* to Petrarch's rigid taste, his insistence on the resolutely allegorical character of Dante's poetry was paramount: it was a showy attempt to lighten the weight of a linguistic prerequisite – the absolute superiority of Latin over the vernacular, as affirmed incessantly by Petrarch – which Dante's opus, evidently, was not able to respect.

On the other hand, Petrarch himself, in his *Fam.* XXI.15, § 1, summing up in a word the guidelines of the Boccaccian exegesis of Dante's *Commedia*, stated: "You ask pardon, somewhat heatedly, for seeming to praise unduly a fellow countryman of ours who is popular for his poetic style but doubtless noble for his theme". This shows that Petrarch recognises the validity of Boccaccio's fundamental argument: the popular garments of the *Commedia* are accompanied by a noble content, which is addressed only to the readers who are adequately prepared for it. But in the words of Petrarch, the emphasis is placed above all on the first attribute, that degrading 'popularity' to which Petrarch obsessively returns in his letter (§§ 10, 14–19, 22).

The relationship between Boccaccio and Petrarch with respect to the evaluation of Dante's work has been studied in depth; it will therefore suffice to briefly recall here only its principal moments.[25] For convenience's sake, let us follow chronological order, restricting ourselves to the most significant events. When Petrarch wrote the *Fam.* XXI.15 in June of 1359, Boccaccio had already composed, apart from the Latin carmen *Ytalie iam certus honos*, the first draft of his biography of Dante as well, the so-called *Trattatello in laude di Dante*. It is a known fact that both works of Boccaccio, the carmen and the biography, were known to Petrarch when he wrote the *Fam.* XXI.15, where indeed, as has already been mentioned, he summarily – but faithfully – repeated the fundamental argument of the two Boccaccian works.[26] But these very works of Boccaccio, and in particular the *Trattatello*, are in their turn dependent on others of Petrarch's texts which contain important reflections on poetry: and this fact is naturally not without its importance. Boccaccio indeed attempts, in the *Trattatello* above all, to interpret Dante's work in light of the criteria employed by Petrarch to define – and defend – true poetry. Putting matters simply, we might say that Boccaccio seeks to disarm Petrarch's anti-Dantism by attempting to demonstrate that Dante's work fits (almost) perfectly with the idea of poetry which Petrarch himself had elaborated.

In Petrarch's judgement, allegory is not one of the possibilities of poetic language but one of the elements that define poetic language as such. In other words, there cannot be poetry without allegory. This principle is already affirmed in the *Africa* (IX 92–97), is amply resumed in the *Collatio laureationis* (§ 9) and further developed in the epistle *Fam.* X.4, addressed by Petrarch to his brother Gherardo, together with the first eclogue of the *Bucolicum carmen, Parthenias*. Here is what Petrarch writes, for example, in *Fam.* X.4, § 2:

> Indeed, what else do the parables of the Savior in the Gospels echo if not a discourse different from ordinary meaning or, to express it briefly, figurative speech, which we call allegory in ordinary language? Yet poetry is woven from this kind of discourse, but with another subject.[27]

The *Fam.* X.4 also contains a famous page on the origins of poetic language. This passage has been much studied, and it is enough to recall a single portion of it. Petrarch explains, as others before him had done (and in particular Isidore of Seville, *Etym.* VIII.7, §§ 1–3), that poetry is first born among primitive men as an elaborate language for addressing the divinities: for this reason, poetry and theology, which is to say sacred language, make use of the same stylistic means. Naturally, this language had to be different from normal language (§ 4): "they [i.e. ancient men] determined to appease the divinity with high-sounding words and to bestow sacred flattery on the divinity in a style far removed from common and public speech". "In addition", Petrarch explains, the early men "employed rhythmical measures in order to provide pleasure and banish tediousness. Indeed it had to be an uncommon form of speech and possess a certain artfulness, exquisiteness, and novelty".

The expressions "different from ordinary meaning" and "removed from common and public speech" confer different shades of meaning on the same notion. Poetry qualifies as a language which is radically different from common language, both on account of its formal characteristics – it is in fact another language with its own rules, which differentiate it radically from spoken language – and on account of the fact that it encloses within itself meanings which are not immediately intelligible and which, if they are to be understood, require special study. As Petrarch explains in *Africa* (IX.92–97), taking up a passage from Macrobius (*In Somn. Scipionis* I.2, §§ 17–21), it is up to the poet, after having established the foundations of the truth, to veil them with an "agreeable" and "varied cloud": this imposes on the reader a comprehensive work of deciphering but also a richer prize once he has attained its solution.

Then what, in Petrarch's view, joins these two aspects – namely, transmission of concepts through allegorical figures and the use of words and stylistic markers which differ from those of spoken language? Certainly, the fact that both of these elements are typical of an elevated language, as is moreover affirmed – though in more generic terms – already by Isidore of Seville (*Etym*. VIII.7, § 2): "[ancient men] raised their praise to the gods, employing splendid words and elegant rhythms".[28] But it might be said that in the eyes of Petrarch, it is important above all that these elements create a radical distance between the language of poetry and that which belongs to common usage. This distance has the purpose not only of limiting access to poetic texts exclusively to those readers who are gifted with an adequate education, but also – and above all – of offering to elevated concepts a stable and immutable form of transmission. Why is the vernacular not suitable to transmit these same concepts? Precisely because it is an irremediably mutable language, incapable, by its very nature, of any stability. Giovanni del Virgilio also confirms this same thing in the carmen directed to Dante which I cited earlier (*Ecl*. I.15–16).[29]

Petrarch adopts and neatly illustrates the same notion in the third of the *Invective contra medicum*, which dates back to the first months of 1353. Petrarch's adversary had maintained that poetry, precisely to the extent it is constituted by words – that is, by elements which are by their nature variable and unstable – cannot be considered a science (§ 67):

> You say that science is fixed and immutable. In this, you don't speak falsely. Then you add that poetry uses meters and vocabulary that vary over time. From this, you conclude that poetry must be excluded from the company of the arts and sciences.[30]

Petrarch at first (partially) accepts the presuppositions on which the argument of his adversary is founded, twisting them however in a sarcastic way against him (§ 69): "Is there any science without words?" Petrarch subsequently however affirms that the Latin poets, as distinguished from all others, succeeded in preserving in their works a substantial linguistic invariability (§§ 81–82): "the Latin poets exhibit no such changes. Which of our poets ever deviated from Virgil's path, with the possible exception of Statius? And even he commands his *Thebaid* to follow the *Aeneid* of Virgil and to worship his footsteps".

Here then is the explanation, in brief, for the reason why Latin is to be considered superior to the vernacular. The devaluation of the vernacular is strictly connected to the conviction that that which is mutable is irremediably inferior to that which is immutable – and this is surely the key point of Petrarchan thought, whose consequences, as we shall see in subsequent chapters of this book, extend also to other aspects of Dante's poem. Rather than being reducible to a fixed formula, to a pure expression of elitism, the contempt for the vernacular is rather that contempt which he who embraces the universal turns upon everything contingent. There is a capital work, in this regard, which transmits to the Middle Ages the ancient Platonic censure of poetry which unconditionally reproduces the instability of life: the *Consolation of Philosophy* of Boethius. The detractors of poetry – including the medic against whom Petrarch addresses himself in the *Invective* – often cite the opening scene of the *Consolation*, in which Philosophy drives the Muses from Boethius' bed, as the passage where the superiority of scientific knowledge over poetry is radically affirmed: the one is stable, the other variable and fickle. Petrarch objects that these readers failed to understand the sense of this Boethian scene: in fact, it is not the Muses of poetry in general who are expelled, but only the Muses of that poetry which takes as its object the world and its passions. And it is not philosophy to drive them out, but the Muse of true poetry – of that poetry, that is, which eschews the instability of worldly things (*Contra med.* III, §§ 116–121).[31]

As has been said, the vernacular is itself, in the eyes of Petrarch, an expression of contingency.[32] For this reason, too, it is considered a language fit to transmit contents which are themselves variable and unstable, subject to becoming: the vernacular is for Petrarch the language of youthful poetry, of that age, that is to say, which is normally 'servant' of passionate impulses. This is a concept which Petrarch repeats various times, toward the end of establishing his self-portrait on principles "of intellectual purification",[33] but also to further signal his distance from Dante. And this too is a critical *topos* with which the ancient commentators of Dante, and Boccaccio foremost among them, will have to come to terms. In the *Prologue* to this book, I cited certain passages from the *Sen.* V.2 (1364), in which Petrarch declares that he early abandoned the project of composing works in the vernacular. Five years before the *Sen.* V.2, Petrarch had affirmed the same thing – but in a rather harsher tone – in his *Fam.* XX.15, § 21: "how true can it be that I am envious of a man [i.e. Dante] who devoted his entire life to those things that were only the flower and first fruits of my youth?" We know that all of this is perfectly false: as is demonstrated by the stratigraphy of manuscript Vat. Lat. 3195, Petrarch worked on the *Rerum vulgarium fragmenta* (*Canzoniere*) up to the last months of his life.[34] But this manifest falsity, at least here, is of secondary importance. What matters is the image that Petrarch offers of himself, which was wholly accepted by his contemporaries, and therefore also the way in which that image interferes with Dante's early critical reception.

Boccaccio perfectly understood the problem posed by Petrarch, and he was not ignorant of the weight that it might have in the assessment of a work like the *Commedia*, which was written in a "common and public speech". In the first draft of the *Trattatello*, Boccaccio translates the pages of Petrarch's

*Fam.* X.4 on the birth of poetry and on the fundamental characteristics of poetic language, thus conferring to Petrarch's ideas, to every appearance, the role of an indispensable conceptual reference point,[35] and Boccaccio would repeat the same operation some twenty years later in his *Esposizioni sopra la "Comedia"* (*ad Inf.* I.73, §§ 73–78).[36] His faithfulness to the source is noteworthy: Boccaccio explains in §§ 130–131 of the *Trattatello* (first draft) that ancient men

> were eager to use words removed from all plebeian or common styles of speech, which would be worthy to be uttered in the presence of the deity. . . . Certainly all this could not be done in a vernacular or ordinary form of speech, but in a way that was artistic, elaborate, and novel.

Boccaccio repeats word for word that which Petrarch had written in *Fam.* X.4, § 4. But, as has rightly been observed, if it is true that poetry cannot be composed "in vernacular form", then the *Commedia* "is not poetry".[37]

The dike which Boccaccio put up against this inevitable conclusion is the very same which I have mentioned: he insisted upon the allegorical, almost esoteric character of Dante's poem. While the linguistic garment of the *Commedia* is popular, its contents are not; and above all, it is not popular in the form through which these contents are transmitted to the reader – an apparently ciphered form, which is not immediately intelligible since it is entrusted to allegorical figures. At least one of the two fundamental criteria posited by Petrarch is therefore respected (*Fam.* X.4, § 2). Boccaccio as an interpreter of Dante strives in this direction, although – and this should be highlighted – he does not at all share Petrarch's devaluation of Dante's vernacular, and in fact, as we shall see, not rarely entertains certain second thoughts on this point. As for the rest, it is known that when it comes to defending poetry, Boccaccio often takes his bearing by Petrarch's ideas only to then sensibly distance himself from them, to such a point that he sometimes even arrives at turning them on their head.[38] Here, however, he is defending Dante rather than poetry in general; Boccaccio thus reveals himself more passive with respect to Petrarch's teaching, because in this case Boccaccio's goal, as has already been stated, is to convince Petrarch of the fact that Dante's work is not unworthy of cultured readers, those dedicated to high poetry.

We therefore return to the question of the allegorical meaning of the *Commedia*: what, finally, is this meaning? What is the occult content of Dante's poem, that content that only the few are permitted to understand? It is above all in confronting this problem that Boccaccio will encounter the greatest difficulties in remaining faithful to his intention to demonstrate the full compatibility of Dante's poem with Petrarch's idea of poetry.

## Oscillations of a Dantist Boccaccio

The principle according to which Dante, in his *Commedia*, adopts an essentially allegorical form of writing is repeated more than once in the *Trattatello*. The most important passage in this regard is located at the end of the biography, when Boccaccio offers to his readers a detailed interpretation of a strange dream which Dante's mother had during her pregnancy – a special dream which foreshadows, among other things, the composition of the *Commedia* (§§ 208–227). I will return to this passage in the third chapter of this book, to examine how one of the *Trattatello*'s early readers who set himself to comment Dante, Benvenuto da Imola, would use it in his annotations to the *Commedia*, attributing to it a meaning exactly contrary to that proposed by Boccaccio. For now, it suffices to mention only a few elements. The dream that Dante's mother had ends with the appearance of a peacock (§ 208), and according to Boccaccio it is this peacock which foreshadows the *Commedia*. The peacock has clumsy and graceless feet and a slow and quiet gait: "ugly feet and silent step" (§ 221). Analogously, the entire 'body' of the *Commedia* is sustained by a language which one cannot but consider "ugly in comparison with the elegant and masterful literary style that every other serious poet employs" (§ 226).

But the peacock, as the bestiaries teach us, has a sweet-smelling flesh which never corrupts (§ 221): "la sua carne è odorifera e incorruttibile", in the original text of the *Trattatello*.[39] Boccaccio explains therefore that the deep sense of the *Commedia* "is symbolically similar to the flesh of the peacock, because whether you give a moral or theological meaning [e.g. allegorical] to any part of the book that you like most, its truth remains simple and immutable". We find the same juxtaposition evoked by Petrarch: Boccaccio counterposes, to a linguistic form which is ungraceful and humble because it is unstable, a substantial truth which is "simple and immutable". But this truth, as the flesh of the peacock, is not evident: it is covered by the rest of the 'body', and is indeed indicated by Boccaccio as "a moral or theological meaning", which is another way of defining its allegorical nature.

Two curious anecdotes contained in the *Trattatello* are also adapted to this principle. The first appears only in the first draft of the work (§ 113): as he is walking through the streets of Verona, Dante accidentally overhears the comments of several ladies who recognise him as the author of the *Inferno*; one of these ladies observes: "Ladies, do you see that man there who goes down to Hell, and comes back whenever he wants to, and brings back news of all those who are down under there?"; and another, with utter ingenuity ("semplicemente"), replies: "Indeed, you must be telling the truth. Don't you see how his beard is singed and his complexion darkened by the heat and the smoke that are down there?". This exchange seems to qualify as a caricatured example of an exegesis which is totally barred from the poetry, totally inadequate for conceiving a deeper level of meaning. It is worth noting that Dante, overhearing the comments of these ladies, smiles to himself, "as though content that they should be of such opinion":[40] as if this episode reassured him of the solidity of the allegorical *integumentum* which he himself conceived to protect the *Commedia* from intellectually unworthy readers.

The comic airiness of the Veronese ladies seems to find a deliberate foil in the discernment of Dino Frescobaldi, "a man of great intellect", who, so soon as he was able to examine the notebook with the first seven cantos of the *Commedia*, which he discovered in Dante's house after the poet had been exiled from Florence,[41] at once recognised the allegorical quality of the texts contained therein (§ 181):

> Dino . . . was impressed no less than the bearer, both because of their beautiful, elegant and ornate style of speech, and also because of the profundity of meaning which he thought that he saw hidden under the lovely cortex of the word.

And it was precisely the allegorical nature of those verses, together with the "ornate style" and their placement, which permitted Frescobaldi to attribute them with certainty to Dante: "For this reason . . . he . . . guessed immediately that they might belong (as in fact they did) to Dante".

It will be noted that Boccaccio, through the eyes of Dino Frescobaldi, defines the "style of speech" of the *Commedia* as "elegant and ornate" ("lo bello e pulito e ornato stile del dire", in the original). This is stated in open contradiction to what he will affirm several paragraphs after, in the chapter on the dream of Dante's mother, where the style of the *Commedia*, as we know, is defined instead as "ugly" ("sozzo", 'dirty', which is the precise opposite of "pulito", 'clean'). Such dissonance should not be surprising. As we mentioned earlier, it is evident that Boccaccio does not share the idea that the vernacular – and Dante's vernacular especially – is "ugly": his is merely a concession to Petrarch, and precisely for this reason it might happen from time to time that he oscillates, or even contradicts himself, whilst expressing his judgement. As a matter of fact, the question of the vernacular constitutes a real obsession for Boccaccio. In the *Genealogie Deorum Gentilium* (XIV.7, § 2), composed between 1350 and the final years of his life, Boccaccio repeats what Petrarch had explained in the *Fam.* X.4: the poets, if they are to be defined as such, must "veil truth in a fair and fitting garment of fiction", and above all they cannot ignore – Boccaccio writes – "the precepts of grammar", that is of Latin. A bit further on into his work,

Boccaccio finds himself forced to define vernacular poetry as an exception with respect to these rules: "I grant that many a man already writes his mother tongue admirably, and indeed has performed each of the various duties of poetry as such".[42] In the epistle of 1371 to Iacopo Pizzinga (*Ep.* XIX), Boccaccio carries this tension to its culmination: Dante, we read in § 26 of the letter, wrote

> in the mother language, but this was not a popular or even rustic language [*non plebeium aut rusticanum*], as some have said; Dante, to the contrary, embellished the mother tongue with artful figures, and in this way rendered the vernacular more beautiful in its meaning than on its surface [*sensu letiorem fecit quam cortice*].[43]

On the one hand, Boccaccio contests those who, like Ilaro – and, of course, Petrarch – had defined Dante's language as 'popular'; on the other, he reiterates that the value of Dante's poetry resides in its sense, rather than in its form. The 'explicit' judgement which Boccaccio passes on the vernacular thus remains uncertain up to the very end. But what is more important still is that a fluctuation of this kind, as we will shortly see, can also be understood in relation to the Boccaccian conception of the *Commedia* as an allegorical poem.

Let us return to the Dino Frescobaldi of Boccaccio's *Trattatello*. Frescobaldi's reaction to his reading of the first seven cantos of the *Inferno* is in part similar and in part different from that of the friar Ilaro. Ilaro negatively judged Dante's choice to write in the vernacular, while Dino to the contrary judges the style of Dante "beautiful, elegant and ornate". Dino, as much as Ilaro, agrees on the other hand that the fundamental meaning of the *Commedia* is hidden under the 'cortex' of the words. But what then is this hidden meaning? In the *Trattatello* Boccaccio does not answer in any clear way. Or rather, he recounts an episode which actually seems to exclude the idea that the *Commedia* might have a hidden meaning. Boccaccio explains (§§ 176–177) that the initial idea to write the *Commedia* came to Dante during the years of his political appointment in Florence (1295–1301), and more precisely in the year 1300, when Dante was 35 years old:[44]

> at a time when he was at his peak in the service of the government of the republic, he gazed out from the heights where he stood and realized from the panoramic view offered by such a place what the life of man is about and what the errors of the masses amount to, and how few there are who do not follow the crowd, and how honorable these few worthy men are; and he studied those who, siding with the crowd, are prone to great confusion, condemning the aspirations of these people

and approving his own far more. There then came into his mind a noble idea: he intended at one time (that is, in a single work) to punish the evildoers with the direst penalties and to honor the virtuous with the highest rewards. . . . After considerable thought about how to do this, in his thirty-fifth year he began to produce what he had a long premeditated: that is, how to rebuke and reward the lives of men according to their various merits. And because he knew that lives are divided into three kinds – that is, the vicious, those who abandon vice and move toward virtue, and the virtuous – he divided his entire work very intelligently into three books, beginning by castigating the vicious life, and ending by rewarding the virtuous one; and he called the whole volume his *Commedia*. . . . And he composed it in the vernacular language with such poetic artistry and with such an impressive and splendid organization that no one has yet been able to find any fault with it.

Let us begin with the end. Boccaccio once more – this time very clearly – praises Dante's vernacular. I have already said that this kind of turnabout should not amaze us – indeed, it demonstrates rather clearly what was Boccaccio's true thought regarding the vernacular and in particular Dante's vernacular. If we reread the passage from another perspective, recalling how Boccaccio interprets the *Commedia* by comparing it to the peacock dreamt by Dante's mother, we find an interesting indication. Boccaccio wrote (§ 226) that the vernacular "is better suited to our present ways of thinking". This is surely an accurate reprise of the argument supporting the choice to write in the vernacular by Ilaro's Dante (§ 11 of the letter): "I put aside the lyre to which I had trusted, and tuned another, in harmony with the tastes of the moderns". Now this choice of accessibility in the passage we have extracted seems to transform into a value. Why did Dante write the *Commedia*? Essentially, to induce men to live in accord with virtue; and to reach this end Dante evidently had to address the public in a way which was immediately comprehensible to them. It is noteworthy that a political meaning is attributed to this operation: even Boccaccio, as Ilaro before him, connects the writing in vernacular to the selection of a public which can concretely act to better the world. Ilaro mentions the fact that Dante intended to address above all men of power ("men of high birth, for whom such works [i.e. poems] were written in a better age", § 11), and Boccaccio widened the *Commedia*'s public to include all of humanity, whilst underlining that it was precisely Dante's political appointment which suggested the composition of a work designed to orient human comportment toward the good.

In full accord with these principles, at §§ 176–177 of the *Trattatello*, Boccaccio explains the sense of Dante's invention in extremely simple terms.

Dante wished "to punish the evildoers with the direst penalties and to honor the virtuous with the highest rewards". The political aim of the work is actuated precisely in virtue of this elementary act of justice. Where, then, is the allegory? Where is the hidden meaning beneath the 'cortex' of the words? Quite simply, there is no such thing; and it is evident that, in this framework, it is perfectly logical that this should be the case. If the *Commedia* was written for the purpose of inducing men to act in a virtuous way, the *Commedia* itself cannot be identified as a text which conceals its fundamental meaning.

The radical oscillation to be found in the *Trattatello* regarding the definition of the representative strategy of Dante's poem reappears twenty years later in the *Esposizioni sopra la "Comedia"*. It will suffice to read a few passages. Above all, the *Esposizioni* generally follow a recurrent schema, and this already is in and of itself significant: a literal explanation is first furnished for each canto of the poem, and then an allegorical explanation. The justification for this exegetic choice is offered in the allegorical exposition of the first canto of the *Inferno*, where Boccaccio makes an effort once more to demonstrate that the *Commedia* is a work possessing a secret meaning. In this case, Boccaccio's argument is bolstered with the chapters of Macrobius' commentary on the *Somnium Scipionis* (1.2, §§ 17–21) in which it is affirmed that the philosophers did not always have recourse to "fables" for no good reason, but that rather, when treating of the soul and of the other subordinate gods, they made use of figurative speech precisely to avoid Nature being exposed without its veils to all glances, including the rudest: "Nature . . . desired to have her secrets handled by more prudent individuals through fabulous narratives".[45] In the same way, Boccaccio continues, the poets who "employ all their skill to follow" the Holy Ghost – which "concealed the lofty secrets of the Divine Mind" – in their turn "concealed behind fabulous speech traces of those things they believed to be most worthy so that what was valuable was not left open to everyone and thus transformed into something common". The reference to Macrobius, beyond being totally consonant with the thesis that Boccaccio proposes to demonstrate, is also, one might say, homage directed at Petrarch: it was indeed precisely Petrarch who cited the same passages of the commentary on the *Somnium Scipionis* in several of his most famous pages, those dedicated to demonstrating that there cannot be poetry without allegory (*Africa* IX.92–97, and above all *Collatio Laureations*, § 9).[46]

This homage to Petrarch had reached its zenith, so to speak, already several pages before, when Boccaccio had categorised Dante's *Commedia* with a profoundly allegorical work like Petrarch's *Bucolicum carmen* (*ad Inf*. I.73, § 77):

> However, Christian poets, of whom there have been many, did not hide in their fabulous speech anything false, especially where they narrated

things dealing with God and the Christian faith. This is plain to see in the work of my excellent teacher Francesco Petrarca, known as the *Bucolics*. If one takes it and opens it – not with envy but with charitable judgment – one will find under its rough bark healthful and extremely pleasant lessons. This is the case with the present work too [i.e. Dante's *Commedia*], as I hope to show in the course of my expositions.[47]

Here another question spontaneously arises: what is the fabulous narration of the *Commedia*, the fantastic invention which, as the mythological tales of Macrobius, hides and protects the truth? Here is how Boccaccio defines the literal sense of Dante's poem, that which supposedly corresponds to a 'fable' (*accessus*, § 8): "its subject in the literal sense, taken simply, is the state of souls after the death of their bodies, insofar as the intention of the entire work's composition deals with and revolves around this topic". This is not an original definition. Boccaccio here is citing another mysterious and elusive document, the so-called *Epistle to Cangrande*, which was, according to some, the work of Dante, and according to others a spurious document. This is not the place to discuss the question of the authenticity of the *Epistle to Cangrande*.[48] What is important to highlight here is that in this definition of the literal sense of the *Commedia*, nothing fabulous can be recognised – in fact, the contrary. And indeed, a few pages before, Boccaccio admitted (*accessus*, § 22):

The substantive plot of this work (i.e., that sinners who die in their sins are condemned to eternal punishment and that those who pass away in the grace of God are raised up to eternal glory) is and has always been true according to the Catholic faith.

The contradiction is utterly apparent and, yet again, is highly revealing. Stubbornly dedicated to demonstrating the allegorical – and therefore sectarian, 'closed', accessible only to the few – character of the *Commedia*, Boccaccio finds himself affirming that Dante's poem contains already in the letter a meaning which "is and has always been true according to the Catholic faith" and therefore nothing fabulous; and thus, no truth hidden by an allegorical narration. We are at the peak of the tension between the genuine idea of Dante matured by Boccaccio on the one hand and his attempt to adapt this idea to Petrarch's positions on the other. It should be emphasised that the dialectic which constitutes the conceptual basis of the entire discourse – that is, the contraposition between that which is mutable and that which is immutable, between the contingent and the universal – is implicitly evoked in this passage. As Boccaccio writes, Dante in his work treats, in the vernacular tongue, of an immutable and eternal truth – indeed, of the most important of all the immutable and eternal truths of the Christian faith: the otherworldly destiny of souls. Such truth is perfectly and fully expressed in the letter of the *Commedia*: the secret and immutable content of the poem, in other words, is not secret. But if this character of immutability emerges already in the letter, this means that everything which belongs to the letter becomes the immediate, and legitimate, vehicle for an immutable and eternal content – including, evidently, the vernacular as well.

## Notes

1 See T. De Robertis, 'Boccaccio copista', in *Boccaccio autore e copista*, ed. by T. De Robertis *et alii* (Mandragora: Florence, 2013), 334.

2 See S. Bellomo, 'Il sorriso di Ilaro e la prima redazione in latino della *Commedia*', *Studi sul Boccaccio* 32 (2004), 205. See also L. Mehus, 'Praefatio', in A. Traversarii, *Latinae epistulae a domino Petro Canneto abbate Camaldulensi . . .* (Florence: Typ. Cesareo, 1759), cccxxi–cccxxii.

3 I quote from the translation of Philip H. Wicksteed, in G. Boccaccio, *Life of Dante*, trans. by P. H. Wicksteed and ed. by W. Chamberlin (Oneworld Classics: Richmond UK, 2009), 105–107. I will cite the original Latin version of Ilaro's letter from B. Arduini and H. Wayne Storey, 'Edizione diplomatico-interpretativa della lettera di frate Ilaro', *Dante Studies* 124 (2006), 77–89. The numeration of the paragraphs follows the scansion proposed by Bellomo, 'Il sorriso di Ilaro', 207–208.

4 See G. Inglese, *Vita di Dante. Una biografia possibile* (Roma: Carocci, 2015), 121–122.

5 Inglese, *Vita di Dante*, 127. Translation mine.

6 The transcription of these lines made by Wicksteed in Boccaccio, *Life of Dante*, 106, contains several small inaccuracies. I therefore here reproduce the text according to Arduini and Wayne Storey, 'Edizione diplomatico-interpretativa', 85. Following is the translation of M. Papio, *Boccaccio's "Expositions" on Dante's "Comedy"*, trans. by M. Papio (Toronto-Buffalo-London: University of Toronto Press, 2009), 52: "I shall sing of the farthest realms, conterminous with the flowing universe, that open wide for the souls and that mete out their rewards according to the merits of each, etc.".

7 See L. C. Rossi, 'La lettera di Ilaro e la tradizione dei commenti', *Studi danteschi* 71 (2006), 265–285.

8 The translation is mine. See G. Boccaccio, *Tutte le opere*, vol. V/1, ed. by V. Branca *et alii* (Milan: Mondadori, 1992), 431. See then M. Eisner, *Boccaccio and the Invention of Italian Literature* (Cambridge: Cambridge University Press, 2013), 12–16.

9 I follow, here and in what follows, the translation of Aldo S. Bernardo: F. Petrarca, *Letters on Familiar Matters, Rerum familiarum libri XVI–XXIV*, trans. by A. S. Bernardo (Baltimore-London: The Johns Hopkins University Press, 1985), 202–207.

10 I quote from L. Bruni, *Le vite di Dante e del Petrarca*, ed. by M. Berté and R. Rognoni, in *Le vite di Dante dal XIV al XVI secolo*, ed. by M. Berté, M. Fiorilla, S. Chiodo and I. Valente (Rome: Salerno, 2017), 244. Translation mine.

11  Bruni, *Le vite di Dante e del Petrarca*, 244.
12  See B. Basile, 'Filippo Villani', in *Censimento dei commenti danteschi*, ed. by
    E. Malato and A. Mazzucchi, vol. 1, *I commenti di tradizione manoscritta (fino
    al 1428)* (Rome: Salerno, 2011), tome 1, 187–191.
13  See the commentary of Bellomo in F. Villani, *Expositio seu Comentum super
    "Comedia" Dantis*, ed. by S. Bellomo (Florence: Le Lettere, 1989), 76 n. 204.
14  All translations of the first commentaries on Dante's poem – with the exception
    of Boccaccio's *Esposizioni* – are mine. See Villani, *Expositio*, 77.
15  See Bellomo, in Villani, *Expositio*, 77 n. 205.
16  Filippo Villani repeats the same thing also in the biography of Dante contained
    in the *De origine civitatis Florentie* (ch. XXII, § 87): see F. Villani, *De origine
    civitatis Florentie et de eiusdem famosis civibus*, ed. by G. Tanturli (Padua: Ant-
    enore Editrice, 1997), 86.
17  See the observations on this point made by Marco Petoletti in D. Alighieri,
    *Epistole, Egloge, Questio de aqua et terra*, ed. by M. Baglio, L. Azzetta, M. Petoletti
    and M. Rinaldi (Rome: Salerno, 2016), 493. As regards the poetic correspon-
    dence between Giovanni del Virgilio and Dante, see the recent study by J. Combs-
    Schilling, 'Tityrus in Limbo: Figures of the Author in Dante's *Eclogues*', *Dante
    Studies* 133 (2015), 1–26. For a general view of the question, see A. R. Ascoli,
    'Blinding the Cyclops: Petrarch after Dante', in *Petrarch & Dante: Anti-Dantism,
    Metaphysics, Tradition*, ed. by Z. Barański and T. J. Cachey (Notre Dame, IN:
    University of Notre Dame Press, 2009), 114–173.
18  I follow the translation of P. H. Wicksteed: *A Translation of The Latin Works of
    Dante Alighieri* (London: J. M. Dent and co., 1904).
19  I use Richard H. Lansing's translation: see *Dante's "Il Convivio"*, trans. by R.
    H. Lansing (New York: Garland, 1990).
20  See Inglese, *Vita di Dante*, 125.
21  See S. Gentili, *L'uomo aristotelico alle origini della letteratura italiana* (Rome:
    Carocci, 2005), 127–165.
22  I cite the translation of Steven Botterill: D. Alighieri, *De vulgari eloquentia*, ed. and
    trans. by S. Botterill (Cambridge-New York: Cambridge University Press, 1996).
23  See E. Auerbach, 'Sacrae Scripturae sermo humilis', *Neuphilologische Mit-
    teilungen* 42 (1941), 57–67. On the variety of languages and styles in the *Com-
    media*, see G. Ledda, *Dante* (Bologna: il Mulino, 2008), 90–93, and *Dante's
    Plurilingualism: Authority, Knowledge, Subjectivity*, ed. by S. Fortuna, M.
    Gragnolati and J. Trabant (London: Legenda, 2010).
24  See Inglese, *Vita di Dante*, 127. Translation mine.
25  See S. Gilson, *Dante and Renaissance Florence* (Cambridge: Cambridge Uni-
    versity Press, 2005), 21–53, E. Filosa, 'To Praise Dante, to Please Petrarch
    (*Trattatello in laude di Dante*)', in *Boccaccio: A Critical Guide to the Complete
    Works*, ed. by V. Kirkham, M. Sherberg and J. Levarie Smarr (Chicago-Lon-
    don: The University of Chicago Press, 2013), 213–220, and the recent works
    of Eisner, *Boccaccio and the Invention of Italian Literature*, and of J. Houston,
    *Building a Monument to Dante: Boccaccio as Dantista* (Toronto: Toronto Uni-
    versity Press, 2016). For a general view, see the essays edited by Z. Barański
    and T. J. Cachey, *Petrarch & Dante: Anti-Dantism, Metaphysics, Tradition*, and
    in particular Cachey, 'Between Petrarch and Dante', 3–49, Ascoli, 'Blinding
    the Cyclops', G. Mazzotta, 'Petrarch's dialogue with Dante', 177–194, and J.
    Steinberg, 'Dante *Estravagante*, Petrarca *Disperso*, and the Spectre of Other
    Woman', 263–289.

26   On the fact that the *Fam.* XXI.15 presupposes Petrarch's acquaintance with the *Trattatello*, see C. Paolazzi, 'Petrarca, Boccaccio e il *Trattatello in laude di Dante*', in *Dante e la "Comedia" nel Trecento* (Milan: Vita e Pensiero, 1989), 151–221.

27   I cite here too from the translation of Aldo S. Bernardo: see F. Petrarca, *Letters on Familiar Matters, Rerum familiarum libri IX–XVI*, trans. by A. S. Bernardo (Baltimore-London: The Johns Hopkins University Press, 1982), 69–75.

28   Translation mine.

29   On Petrarch's acquaintance with the poetic exchange between Giovanni del Virgilio and Dante, see Ascoli, 'Blinding the Cyclops', 137–142.

30   I quote David Marsh's translation: see F. Petrarch, *Invectives*, ed. and trans. by D. Marsh (Cambridge, MA-London, England: The I Tatti Renaissance Library-Harvard University Press, 2003).

31   See S. Gentili, 'La nature de la poésie et la solitude des poètes de Pétrarque à Boccace', in *Boccace humaniste latin*, ed. by H. Casanova Robin, S. Gambino Longo and F. Labrasca (Paris: Garnier, 2016), 303–321.

32   For a wider investigation on Petrarch's reflection on Latin and vernacular, see S. Rizzo, 'Petrarca, il latino e il volgare', *Quaderni petrarcheschi* 7 (1990), 7–40.

33   S. Gentili, 'La malinconia nel Medioevo: dal *Problema* 30.1 di Aristotele a *Donna me prega* di Cavalcanti al sonetto 35 di Petrarca', *Bollettino di Italianistica* 7/2 (2010), 156. Translation mine.

34   For a deft synthesis of the principal studies on the drafting history of the *Canzoniere*, see R. Antonelli, '*Rerum vulgarium fragmenta* di Francesco Petrarca', in *Letteratura Italiana. Le opere*, ed. by A. Asor Rosa, 4 vols. (Turin: Einaudi, 1992), vol. 1, 349–471, and L. Marcozzi, 'Making the *Rerum vulgarium fragmenta*', in *The Cambridge Companion to Petrarch*, ed. by A. Russell Ascoli and U. Falkeid (Cambridge: Cambridge University Press, 2015), 51–62.

35   On the use of *Fam.* X.4 in the *Trattatello*, see T. Ricklin, 'Les *vetulae* et les fables dans les *Genealogie Deorum Gentilium*: Boccace entre Pétrarque et Dante', in *Ut philosophia poesis. Questions philosophiques dans l'oeuvre de Dante, Pétrarque et Boccace*, ed. by J. Biard and F. Mariani Zini (Paris: Vrin, 2008), 191–211. I will use Vincenzo Zin Bollettino's translation of Boccaccio's *Trattatello*: see G. Boccaccio, *The Life of Dante*, trans. by V. Zin Bollettino (New York-London: Garland, 1990).

36   See L. C. Rossi, 'Presenze di Petrarca in commenti danteschi fra Tre e Quattrocento', *Aevum* 70/3 (1996), 445–446.

37   G. Tanturli, 'Il disprezzo per Dante dal Petrarca al Bruni', *Rinascimento* s. 2/25 (1985), 203. Translation is mine.

38   On this, see M. Eisner, 'A Singular Boccaccio: Defending Poetry in the *Decameron* and in the *Genealogie*', *Quaderni d'italianistica* 38/2 (2017), 179–199.

39   See Boccaccio, *Vita di Dante*, ed. by P. G. Ricci (Milan: Mondadori, 2002²), 59.

40   I follow here the translation of Philip H. Wicksteed (Boccaccio, *Life of Dante*, 37), because Zin Bollettino's distorts the sense of Boccaccio's words. Boccaccio writes: "Le quali parole udendo egli dir dietro a sé, e conoscendo che da pura credenza delle donne venivano, piacendogli, e quasi contento che esse in cotale oppinione fossero, sorridendo alquanto, passò avanti"; and Zin Bolettino translates: "Dante, hearing these words behind him, and knowing that they were spoken by naive women in perfectly good faith, was pleased that they should have *such a high opinion of him*, and, smiling a bit, he proceeded on his way", attributing to Dante a judgement on the sense of the lady's observation which is absent in the original Boccaccian text and altogether inappropriate.

41   On this legend, which has come down to us only through Boccaccio, see Inglese, *Vita di Dante*, 92–98.

42 I quote Charles Osgood's translation: see *Boccaccio on Poetry* (New York: The Liberal Arts Press Inc., 1956²).

43 Boccaccio, *Tutte le opere*, vol. V/1 666. Translation is mine. On these passages, see G. Tanturli, 'Il Petrarca a Firenze: due definizioni della poesia', *Quaderni petrarcheschi* 9–10 (1992–1993), 143–145.

44 As other ancient commentators, Boccaccio too holds that the year in which Dante began to write the poem was the same in which the tale is set, which is to say, 1300: see on this S. Bellomo, '"La natura delle cose aromatiche" e il sapore della *Commedia*', *Critica del testo* 14/1 (2011), 538–540. In truth, it is known that the composition of the *Commedia* began later, probably in 1308 or in the first months of 1309 (Inglese, *Vita di Dante*, 102–103).

45 I quote the translation of William Harris Stahl: see Macrobius, *Commentary on the Dream of Scipio*, trans. by W. Harris Stahl (New York: Columbia University Press, 1952).

46 The passage of Macrobius is presupposed also in vv. 23–29 of Boccaccio's carmen *Ytalie iam certus honos*.

47 The association between the *Commedia* and the *Bucolicum carmen* had already been proposed by Boccaccio, on the basis of the same arguments, in the *Geneal. Deor. Gent.* XIV.8, § 22.

48 There is an endless bibliography on this question. See the edition of Luca Azzetta, in D. Alighieri, *Epistole, Egloge, Questio de aqua et terra*, which is preceded by a broad introduction with an up-to-date bibliographical summary (273–276).

# 2 Interpreting Dante in the shadow of Petrarch and Boccaccio

## The interpreters of the *Commedia* in the late thirteenth century

Some months before starting his first series of lessons on the *Commedia*, Benvenuto da Imola wrote to Petrarch, requesting his aid in resolving certain profound doubts of his. Why was poetry not included among the seven liberal arts? And above all: why did Boethius, in the *Consolation of Philosophy*, express such strong hostility toward the poets? Benvenuto's letter was lost, but we have Petrarch's answer. This is the *Sen.* XV.11, penned in Padua on 9 February 1374.[1] Thus, in all likelihood Benvenuto wrote to Petrarch toward the end of 1373 or a bit before. In the same months, Benvenuto was attending the public lectures given by Boccaccio on the *Commedia*, which had been commissioned by the Florence municipality. About a year after, in 1375, Benvenuto would hold his first course on Dante's poem in Bologna. In other words, the exegetic activity of the most important of Dante's fourteenth-century commentators stands directly – and deliberately – beneath the sign of Petrarch and Boccaccio.

As I indicated in the *Prologue*, Benvenuto da Imola is not the first Dante interpreter to make explicit reference to Boccaccio and to Petrarch in his commentary on the *Commedia*. Before him, there was the Neapolitan Guglielmo Maramauro, who in the preface to his own commentary asserts that Boccaccio and Petrarch helped him to interpret Dante.[2] Maramauro wrote his commentary in a little more than four years, between 1369 and 1373;[3] Boccaccio started his public lectures on the *Commedia* on 23 October 1373, and we do not know if Maramauro was able to attend Boccaccio's lessons on Dante. But even if he was, it seems improbable that Maramauro had the time to capitalise on what he had learned from Boccaccio's living voice, given that Maramauro finished his own commentary on the *Commedia*, as has already been said, more or less in the same period when Boccaccio commenced his *lectura Dantis* in Florence.

However, there are some points of contact between Maramauro's comment and the *Esposizioni* of Boccaccio, as we shall see. This demonstrates that the two of them had certainly had a chance to discuss the interpretation of certain passages of Dante's poem, either during their meetings in Naples or in other towns.[4] For his part, Benvenuto da Imola certainly attended Boccaccio's lessons on Dante: Benvenuto himself mentions it on several occasions in his commentary. But Benvenuto could not have read the *Esposizioni*, which were published only after his death. It is most likely however that Benvenuto preserved some notes from those lessons and that he used them in his commentary. Moreover, Benvenuto, like Maramauro, also had a relationship of friendship and close confidence with Boccaccio: some passages of Benvenuto's commentary are therefore explicitly tied to suggestions which issued from Boccaccio's own mouth.[5] Benvenuto also read and widely employed the other fundamental Dantean work by Boccaccio, the *Trattatello in laude di Dante*, both of whose drafts he knew,[6] while it appears that the *Trattatello* was unknown to Maramauro.[7]

Other Dante commentators from the end of the fourteenth century show a more or less strong proximity to Boccaccio: Francesco da Buti, the so-called Anonimo Fiorentino and Filippo Villani.[8] All of them were very familiar with the work that Boccaccio had dedicated to the interpretation of Dante. In contrast to Maramauro and Benvenuto, they could read the *Esposizioni*, and they used them liberally in their comments – at least up to the first verses of canto XVII of the *Inferno*, beyond which point, as is known, the *Esposizioni* of Boccaccio do not continue, since Boccaccio died long before finishing his work.

In the previous chapter, I brought to light the tensions that thread throughout Boccaccio's interpretive work on Dante. The questions which we must answer now are thus the following: How did the first readers of Boccaccio's works on Dante react to these tensions? Were they able to discern them, and if so, did they comprehend their origin? Which of the two 'dissonant' lines that characterise Boccaccio's Dantean work – namely, that which aims at emphasising the allegoric dimension of Dante's writing, on the one hand, and that which by contrast tends to recognise the full autonomy of the literal sense of the *Commedia* on the other – did they privilege in their commentaries? And above all: were these readers also readers of Petrarch? Were they therefore able to directly confront Petrarch's thoughts on poetry? And, if so, did they reach the point of elaborating autonomous reflections on Dante's poetry, or, as in Boccaccio's case, did the intention to defend Dante from Petrarch's devaluation prevail in them?

Let us begin with the first Dantean interpreter who makes explicit reference to Petrarch and Boccaccio in his commentary on the *Commedia*: Guglielmo Maramauro. A Neapolitan, son of a family of noble origin,

Maramauro probably was born around 1318. His career as an official of the Angevin monarchy allowed him to travel in Italy and abroad. In the last years of his life Maramauro taught at the University of Naples, where he gave courses on the work of Thomas Aquinas. He was still a teacher when he died. The precise date of his passing is not known, but must fall somewhere between 1379 and 1383.[9] By reason of his mobility and his social status, Maramauro had frequent contact with the Tuscan cultural world, whose most prestigious and influential representatives he certainly knew. In the passage of the *Prologo* in which Petrarch and Boccaccio are cited, two other relevant names appear: "I began this difficult task with the help of Messer Giovanni Boccaccio and Messer Francesco Petrarca, and of parson Forese and Messer Bernardo Scannabecchi".

It is not possible to establish what contribution Forese Donati and Bernardo Scannabecchi made to Maramauro's interpretative work. Indeed, it was assumed that the names of the two literati – together with the still more high-sounding names of Petrarch and Boccaccio – were quoted by Maramauro only in order to provide prestige to his own work.[10] While the actual relationships between Maramauro, Forese Donati and Bernardo Scannabecchi remain difficult to determine, there is no doubt, on the other hand, that Maramauro personally knew Boccaccio and Petrarch.

## Poetry, allegory, the vernacular: 'mechanical' marks

I will return shortly to the presence of Boccaccio in Maramauro's commentary on the *Commedia*. First, it is necessary to gain a more thorough knowledge of the relation between the Neapolitan commentator and the most unexpected of the persons mentioned in the *Prologo* of his commentary, Petrarch. Maramauro, as we know, states that Petrarch helped him in the "difficult task" of commenting Dante. Can we believe him? In part we can, and in part we cannot. It is altogether far-fetched to suppose that Petrarch offered advice on the interpretation of the *Commedia* – it is well known that Petrarch expressed an aversion toward Dante, going so far as to declare that he did not know the *Commedia*: "I have never possessed his book", we read in the *Fam.* XXI.15, § 10, a document that is a fundamental testimony for the kind of relationship that Petrarch wanted to establish with Dante's work, as we have observed in the previous chapter.[11] In any case, it is certain that Petrarch and Maramauro had the chance to meet each other and to visit one another. The two *Seniles* letters (XI.5 e XV.4) that Petrarch sent to Maramauro testify to the fact: beyond the formulae attributable to a rhetorical use, an authentic affection and even a remarkable esteem is perceptible in both the epistles ("you have set me down in the midst of the events, which is the mark of a superhuman intellect").[12] Most of all, Maramauro had some familiarity with Petrarch's work, both in Latin and the vernacular.

This is demonstrated by two explicit quotations in his commentary, one from the *Africa* (*ad Inf.* I.10–12), the other from the *Rerum vulgarium fragmenta* (*ad Inf.* VIII.1–12).[13]

Let us come now to the issue that most interests us: Was Maramauro aware of the tension that characterises the relation between Boccaccio and Petrarch regarding the interpretation of Dante? Was Maramauro also, like Boccaccio, forced to insist upon the allegoric quality of Dante's writing in order to defend the *Commedia* from the accusation of its being a 'popular' work? At first glance, one would be tempted to say not. In contrast to Boccaccio, Maramauro never proposes a general reflection on the *Commedia*'s language: he proceeds rather to comment the poem step by step, verse for verse, and he therefore tends to enhance the allegoric dimension of Dante's writing only when it is opportune to do so. In other words, he does not do so systematically. For example, when, at the beginning of his comment on the first canto of the *Commedia*, Maramauro writes that "this first chapter is wholly allegorical, which is to say it contains a meaning different from the literal one",[14] he obviously intends to underline that this is not the case for the entire poem, but only for some of its parts, among which the first canto. Moreover, there is no doubt that the first canto of the poem is an allegorical canto: all of the figuration – from the famous "dark wood" (v. 1) to the hill illuminated by the sun (vv. 13–18), up to the three beasts (vv. 31–59) and the mysterious "greyhound" announced by Virgil (vv. 101–112)[15] – has evidently a 'double' value.[16] To affirm that the first canto of the *Commedia* is "wholly allegorical", in other words, is appropriate, and indeed in its way actually necessary; in and of itself, it cannot be taken to possess any apologetic value.

What Maramauro states in the margins of another allegorical – indeed declaredly allegorical – passage of Dante's poem is, on the other hand, more interesting. In canto IX of the *Inferno*, Dante and Virgil find themselves in difficulty; the infernal city of Dis is guarded by terrible demons, "the ferocious Erinyes" (v. 45) that block the travellers' way. The impasse is broken by the arrival of a mysterious emissary of Paradise, a sort of angel who throws open Dis' doors, overwhelming the resistance of the demons and thus allowing Dante and Virgil to continue with their voyage (vv. 61–106). The appearance of the 'heavenly' emissary is preceded by a famous appeal to the reader (vv. 61–63):

> O you who have sound intellects,
> gaze on the teaching that is hidden
> beneath the veil of the strange verses.

Together with a passage of canto VIII of the *Purgatorio* (vv. 19–21), this is the most direct premonition that Dante offers to his reader regarding the presence of an allegoric meaning: and it is well to observe that in both these cases we are speaking of a series of warnings referring to a limited portion of the poem, not to the poem as a whole. How does Maramauro comment on the appeal of canto IX of the *Inferno*? He comments on it in a way that is very interesting for us:

> This passage is intended to those who, by exerting themselves and studying, attempt to identify [in the *Commedia*] the poetry, which is to say the passages which are properly poetic, in which the contents take on a different aspect as compared to what appears in the letter; the poetic passages have in point of fact numerous meanings, which differ from one another. And Dante states all of this because this canto is particularly poetic, as indeed is his entire work; and Dante says as much against those that wish to denigrate his work, saying that there is no hidden meaning in it.[17]

Here we do perceive an apologetic tone. Indeed, the apologetic intention of the commentator is fully explicit. First of all, it is important to pay attention to his word choice: Maramauro uses the word "poetry" ("poesia") as synonymous with "allegory"; indeed, Maramauro writes that poetry necessarily implies a 'polysemy', a plurality of meanings. It is Petrarch, certainly not Dante, who on several occasions guarantees the identity between poetry and allegory, as we have observed in the previous chapter. In the *Collatio laureationis* (§ 9), Petrarch writes, for example, that the fundamental task of the poet – or rather, what distinguishes his kind of language from every other – is the use of figurative speech that does not render the truth immediately evident;[18] and in *Fam.* X.4, § 12, referring to the first eclogue of his *Bucolicum carmen*, *Parthenias*, Petrarch adds that "its nature is such that it must be explained by the author himself to be understood".[19] Is Petrarch therefore the inspiration for this comment by Maramauro? No, the inspiration is Boccaccio – a Boccaccio who is evidently concerned, here as elsewhere, with adapting the poetry of Dante to Petrarch's rules. It was indeed Boccaccio alone, among the interpreters of the fourteenth century, who dwelt on the appeal to the readers of *Inf.* IX 61–63 so as to defend Dante from the mysterious detractors that "deny that the author intended anything other than simply what is contained in their literal meaning" – the same detractors to whom even Maramauro refers. Boccaccio wrote:

> These words of the author directly contradict those who, unable to grasp what is hidden under the veil of these verses, deny that the author intended anything other than simply what is contained in their literal meaning. This passage allows such people to understand clearly that

the author did in fact represent more than what may be seen on the surface. The author calls these verses of his 'strange', inasmuch as no one before him had ever composed such a fiction in vernacular verses, but always literal ones. Thus, these verses seem 'strange', insofar as they are unaccustomed to such a style.[20]

The reference to Dante's detractors is resumed in the same terms by Maramauro. It is beyond any doubt, in other words, that in this case Maramauro adopts an observation from Boccaccio as his own (perhaps Boccaccio shared this observation with Maramauro during one of their meetings, or – but this is less likely, as I have already said – Maramauro took it from his attendance at the *lectura Dantis* held by Boccaccio in Florence). But who were these detractors? We do not know: none of the commentators prior to Boccaccio formulates a similar accusation to that reported in this passage. Certainly, from the perspective of Boccaccio/Petrarch, to deny the presence of an allegoric meaning in Dante's verses means to exclude the *Commedia* from the category of poetic works. And even on this Maramauro appears perfectly in agreement with his source, so much so that he uses the term "poetry", as we have seen, as if it were a synonym of "allegory".

However, Maramauro, in contrast with Boccaccio, fails to clarify what the allegoric meaning is "that is hidden beneath the veil of the strange versets". The reference to a hidden meaning remains, however, undeveloped, which shows that Maramauro's reuse of Boccaccio's reflections does not imply conscious acquiescence to an idea: it is rather more like to a mechanical mark, deprived of effective interpretative consequences. It is very unlikely, on the other hand, that Maramauro was capable of grasping the underlying reasons for Boccaccio's commentary on *Inf.* IX 61–63. I have underlined this several times: whenever he has the opportunity to do so, Boccaccio highlights the allegorical dimension of the *Commedia* to compensate for the fact that it is written in vernacular – in a language, that is, which some readers, and Petrarch above all, believe unworthy of a cultivated public. Indeed, not by chance is the 'problem' of the vernacular mentioned by Boccaccio in a totally explicit way even in his gloss on *Inf.* IX. 61–63. According to Boccaccio, Dante, using the term "strange" in reference to his own "versets" (v. 63), was admitting to his awareness of the fact that "no one before him had ever composed such a fiction in vernacular verses, but always literal ones" ("literal" – "litterali" in the original version[21] – means in fact 'in Latin'). Maramauro, on the other hand, does not at all refer to the question of the superiority of Latin over the vernacular and to the problems that the choice to write in the vernacular might bring with it; he refers to this neither in the comment on *Inf.* IX, 61–63, nor elsewhere. Maramauro, after all, has no direct knowledge of Petrarch the 'theoretician of poetry': Maramauro's

Petrarch is in the first place Petrarch the poet – a poet who does not disdain, moreover, the vernacular language.

A somewhat richer portrait can be painted from the work of another ancient interpreter of the *Commedia*, who wrote some three decades after Maramauro, namely between the end of the fourteenth century and the first years of the fifteenth. I am talking about an author whose identity is unknown and who is therefore indicated as the 'Anonimo Fiorentino' on account of his origin, or else as the 'Anonimo Fanfani', from the name of his first modern editor.[22] Of the life of the Anonimo Fiorentino, we know little. Indeed, self-biographical references are missing in his commentary; his geographic origin is inferred, hypothetically, only from the fact that he shows a special interest in the history of Florence, particularly its recent history.[23] He is in any case a 'minor' author, gifted with a good literary culture but incapable of elaborating an original reading of the *Commedia*; his commentary – which, incidentally, had a minimum diffusion[24] – is strongly indebted to his predecessors. As I have indicated above, the Anonimo Fiorentino was very familiar with Boccaccio's *Esposizioni sopra la "Comedia"*, and indeed he makes abundant use of them in his commentary. But the Anonimo Fiorentino also, like Maramauro before him, does not seem able to grasp the tensions that agitate the interpretation of the *Commedia* proposed by Boccaccio, despite his having direct access, unlike his Neapolitan colleague, to some of the most important works by Petrarch the 'theoretician of poetry' – indeed, to the same works that put the 'Dantist' Boccaccio so hard to the test.[25]

## Other isolated pieces: the commentary of the Anonimo Fiorentino

The Anonimo Fiorentino commences his commentary by immediately tackling a subject of great importance: the question of the language in which the *Commedia* is written, the vernacular. And he does this by recounting an episode that is by now familiar to us. The commentary of the Anonimo Fiorentino opens with this report:

> The author originally began his tripartite poem, the *Commedia*, with these verses in Latin: 'Ultima regna canam fluido contermina mundo, | Spiritibus quae lata patent, quae praemia solvunt | Pro meritis cuicumque suis', etc. And he had already written a goodly part of the poem when he changed his mind, after realising that the nobles and other powerful men had already almost completely abandoned liberal and philosophical studies, and that almost none of them dedicated themselves now to cultivating knowledge; and when they still did, they

exclusively employed works translated into the vernacular. For this reason, the author, desiring to obtain glory for his work and knowing that this glory might be granted only by powerful men, who since ancient times had rendered poets famous, decided to write his extraordinary poem in a language that at least superficially conformed with the education and the intelligence of the powerful men of his time. He therefore abandoned the Latin verses and began in vernacular.[26]

We well know the origin of this tale: it comes from the letter of the mysterious friar Ilaro, which we considered at some length in the previous chapter. Naturally, the Anonimo Fiorentino did not know of Ilaro's letter as such: as I have said, before the eighteenth century nobody except Boccaccio had access to this document. The report in the passage cited derives from the principal source of the Anonimo Fiorentino's commentary, Boccaccio's *Esposizioni*. If we carefully compare the two passages, Boccaccio's with that of the Anonimo Fiorentino, we will note an interesting difference. I have already transcribed the passage of the Anonimo Fiorentino's comment; let us now read the page from Boccaccio that Anonimo Fiorentino kept open on his desk as he was writing the *Proemio* of his commentary:

we must now clear up one last question before beginning the lectures, one that has been posed frequently, and especially by learned men. These men ask: 'It is everyone's opinion that Dante was a highly cultured man; but if he was so cultured, why did he decide to write such a praiseworthy work in the vernacular?'. To such a query, it seems to me that one may answer thus: there is no doubt that Dante was an extremely erudite man, above all regarding poetry, and he was desirous of fame, as all of us are generally. He began this work in Latin verses:

Ultima regna canam fluvido contermina mundo,
spiritibus que lata patent, que premia solvent
pro meritis cuicunque suis, etc.

And he proceeded somewhat further as well before making up his mind to change its style. The reasoning that convinced him sprang from the knowledge that liberal arts and philosophy had been completely abandoned by kings, rulers, and other respectable men who once were accustomed to honouring and immortalizing famous poets and their works. Therefore, seeing Virgil and others almost entirely forgotten or in the hands of plebeians and men of low rank, he realised that the same thing would happen to his work and consequently decided not to allow what he was spending so much energy on to be subjected to the same fate. As a result, he resolved to adapt his poem, at least on its external surface, to the intelligence of his contemporaries.

As can be seen, the Anonimo Fiorentino does not repeat this passage entirely. He sums up Boccaccio's tale here and there, and he eliminates the first paragraph, in which Boccaccio reports the critiques that some had levelled against Dante. The friar Ilaro declared his surprise at the fact that Dante had written his poem in the vernacular, but he never called into question whether this occurred because of Dante's incapacity to write in Latin. As we know, however, it was Petrarch who expressed a genuinely negative judgement on Dante's Latin (*Fam.* XXI.15, § 24). It is evident, in short, that in Boccaccio's *Esposizioni* the report preserved in Ilaro's letter serves to confute those who, like Petrarch, held that Dante might well have been incapable of grappling with the language of the classics. The efforts of Boccaccio, however, did not bring an end to the problem. As we have seen in the previous chapter, Filippo Villani would use the legend of Ilaro precisely to demonstrate that Dante had been the first to recognise his inability to write an entire poem in Latin hexameters.

Why does the Anonimo Fiorentino eliminate Boccaccio's reference to the criticism levelled against Dante "by learned men"? We do not know, and it is difficult to formulate a hypothesis in this regard. While the causes for the Anonimo Fiorentino's silence about this portion of Boccaccio's passage remain unknown, we can however try to reflect on the consequences thereof. By remaining silent on the suspicion formulated by some readers regarding Dante's ability to write in Latin, the Anonimo Fiorentino – at least partially – stultifies the ideological weight of Ilaro's tale. The report of the original edition in Latin of the *Commedia* ends up appearing mere isolated information, useful for explaining why Dante wrote his poem in vernacular but not why this choice was, in the judgement of some readers, surprising and therefore in need of special justification.

The reflection on the inferiority of the vernacular as compared to Latin had a great weight in the dialogue between Boccaccio and Petrarch regarding the *Commedia* and, even before then, in the confrontation between Giovanni del Virgilio and Dante himself. In the commentary of the Anonimo Fiorentino, every reference to this reflection disappears. This is interesting because, in contrast with Maramauro, the Anonimo Fiorentino is very familiar with some of the most important pages that Petrarch had dedicated to the 'theory' of poetical composition; and, as we know, Petrarch the 'theoretician of poetry' expresses himself in exclusively negative terms about poetry in the vernacular. In the previous chapter we focused especially on the *Fam.* X.4 and more precisely on the passages dedicated to the origin of poetry, in which Petrarch claims that poetry was born as a language radically different from those normally used by men. I then mentioned the pages of the *Collatio laureationis* and of the *Invective contra medicum* in which Petrarch asserts the identity between poetry and allegory. Now, all these works were directly known to the Anonimo Fiorentino. The *Fam.* X.4 is explicitly quoted by the Anonimo Fiorentino two times, in the comment on cantos I and XXI of the *Purgatorio*. Let us consider the first of these quotations. The Anonimo Fiorentino focuses on the invocation to the Muses in verses 7–12, and he writes:

> *O holy Muses.* He invokes, according to the custom of the poets, the nine muses; and he calls them 'holy' because the poetic art was born to offer praises and sacrifices to God, as Petrarch explains in one of his letters: "they determined to appease the divinity with high-sounding words and to bestow sacred flattery on the divinity in a style far removed from common an public speech; in addition they employed rhythmical measures," etc.[27]

We are already quite familiar with the passage of the *Fam.* X.4 quoted by the Anonimo Fiorentino. Boccaccio, too, uses it on several occasions, both in the *Trattatello* (first draft, §§ 128–137; second draft, §§ 81–85) and in the *Esposizioni sopra la "Comedia"*. In the *Esposizioni* in particular, Boccaccio translates the words of Petrarch in the comment on *Inf.* I.73, in an annotation that contains another long excursus on the birth of poetry. As regards the fundamental core of Petrarch's tale, the birth of poetic language beginning from the search for a language capable of overcoming the instability of 'natural' language, Boccaccio expands on his source, writing:

> [The ancient Greeks] recognized that during the offering of sacrifices it was necessary to enunciate some words containing their prayers to God and words of praise worthy of Him. Knowing that it was not appropriate when addressing such a Deity to utter familiar words like those we use to speak to our friends or those used between master and servant, they mandated that the priests, who were especially chosen and worthy men, find words that were proper.

This is a concept to which we have returned many times. And indeed we are very familiar by now with how Boccaccio reacts to the problem that necessarily arises in light of the observation that Dante does not disdain to use "familiar words like those we use to speak to our friends" in his verses. Several lines after, Boccaccio adds: "The speech that comprised the high mysteries of the Divinity was uttered in such a way, concealing them beneath a poetic veil, as to prevent them from losing their great value among the people on account of excessive familiarity". It is interesting to observe that the Anonimo Fiorentino, even when reading the *Fam.* X.4 and Boccaccio's *Esposizioni*, gives no sign of having noticed the tension which emerges when one applies the rule about poetic language proposed by Petrarch to the *Commedia*. In his comment on *Inf.* I.73, rather than reproducing Boccaccio's excursus from *Fam.* X.4, the Anonimo Fiorentino cuts to the chase: "*Poeta fuit et cantai*. Here Virgil introduces himself and says that he was a poet; and that he wrote the story of Aeneas, who came to Italy from Troy and was the son of Anchises and the goddess Venus". And then the Anonimo Fiorentino continues, not by offering a discussion on the birth of poetry, as Boccaccio does, but rather a detailed summary of the narrative content of the *Aeneid*.[28]

To all evidence, the Anonimo Fiorentino does not consider the vernacular inferior to Latin; nor, probably, does he perceive the first as irreparably mutable and the second as stable and immutable. And while he also grasps this substantial difference between the two languages, he gives no sign of considering literature in vernacular language *ipso facto* inferior to that in Latin. The Anonimo Fiorentino was moreover a fine connoisseur of the vernacular poetry produced in Italy between the thirteenth and the fourteenth centuries.[29] He had read – and freely quotes in his commentary on Dante – the vernacular masterpieces of Boccaccio and Petrarch, the *Decameron* and the *Rerum vulgarium fragmenta*, as we shall see later.

Perhaps precisely because of his immunity to the devaluation of the vernacular promoted by Petrarch, the Anonimo Fiorentino does not confer any peculiar value to the allegoric dimension of Dante's writing. Although he employs Boccaccio's *Esposizioni*, he does not relay the bipartite structure according to which the allegorical interpretation systematically follows the literal interpretation. Like Maramauro, the Anonimo Fiorentino seems rather to consider allegory as one of the possibilities of the *Commedia*'s poetic language, not as its specific and unifying characteristic. This too is an element worth noting, above all if it is evaluated in the light of the other explicit quotation from Petrarch, the 'theoretician of poetry', which is contained in the commentary of the Anonimo Fiorentino.

Let us examine it. We are in canto XXV of the *Inferno*. Describing the metamorphosis of the thieves into horrible hybrid monsters (*Inf.* XXV.49– 151), Dante directly addresses the great classical poets that ventured the narration of similar events, stating (vv. 94–99):

> Let Lucan now be silent, where he touches on
> miserable Sabellus and Nasidius,
> and let him listen to what the bow now looses.
> About Cadmus and Arethusa let Ovid be silent,

for if in his poetry he converts him into a serpent
and her into a fountain, I do not envy him.[30]

Reading these verses, the Anonimo lingers on the expression "converte poetando",[31] "in his poetry he converts":

*In his poetry he converts*. The poets create fictions to entertain their readers and to involve them in the sweetness of style. The fables of the poets do not erase the truth, but they enrich it through fictions. As Petrarch says, "the task of the poets is not to supplant truth with false stories, but to give truth a different form through figurations that are not immediately intelligible, and to adorn these with a more beautiful and cultivated style than the common".[32]

The Anonimo Fiorentino might have taken the passage from Petrarch's *Collatio laureationis* (§ 9),[33] or else from the first of the *Invective contra medicum*, where we read (§ 160):[34] "In the first book of his *Institutes*, he [e.g. Lactantius] writes: 'the poet's function consists in translating actual truths into different forms using indirect and figural language with a certain decorum'".[35] As these words evince, Petrarch is not elaborating anything new or original; he is simply citing a page of Lactantius (*Inst.* I.11). In any case, this is a concept of some importance, and one that Petrarch, as we know, often repeats: there is no poetry without allegorical transfiguration of the 'truth'; to transmit the truth without recourse to an 'indirect and figural language' means to make something other than poetry. In the context of the *Collatio laureationis*, but above all in the first *Invectiva contra medicum*, the words of Lactantius are cited with a clear defensive intent. Indeed, in the *Invectiva*, Petrarch responds to an accusation that one of his interlocutors had addressed to the poets insofar as they are the creators of fictions (§§ 153–154):

With the astounding temerity of a lowly craftsman, you condemn these fictions and all others of this kind as contradicting the truth. Yet they contain a judicious and delightful allegorical sense which is purposely hidden from you and your ilk.

To reinforce this thesis, Petrarch cites Lactantius, as we have seen, and a little later on adds (§ 164):

the poets . . . strive to adorn the truths of the world with beautiful veils. In this way, the truth eludes the ignorant masses. . . . But for perceptive and diligent readers, it is just as delightful to discover as it is difficult to find.

What does the Anonimo take from Petrarch's words? Does he fully understand their implications, and does he form therefrom a general principle of exegesis for Dante's poetry?

Before responding to this question, it is necessary to emphasise a banal error of interpretation committed by the Anonimo Fiorentino. When Dante, referring to Ovid, writes "in his poetry he converts", he is not referring in the least to the 'transformation' of a truth through the employment of fictions, but he rather alludes – and, what is more, wholly explicitly – to a genuine transformation, to be understood in a literal sense. In the *Metamorphoses*, Ovid indeed collects myths that conclude with the transformation of their protagonists: in the two cases recalled by Dante, "Cadmus and Arethusa" transform respectively "into a serpent" (*Met*. IV.563–604) and "into a fountain" (*Met*. V.572–641). The citation of Petrarch thus appears to lack all motive. Perhaps the Anonimo Fiorentino was misled by the 'meta-literary' tone of the passage which he was reading and so ended up extending it as well to an expression which he should rather have interpreted in much simpler and more 'immediate' terms. But it is more probable that the juxtaposed use of the words "poetry" ("poetando") and "converts" ("converte") spontaneously evoked in him the memory of a theoretical principle on poetry which Petrarch had formulated. It is however evident that this principle, cited as it is cited by the Anonimo Fiorentino, appears to be strongly simplified: that is to say, it loses both its original apologetic value and, above all, its general hermeneutic weight.

The sentence passed by Petrarch-Lactantius on the "indirect and figural language" of poetry, inserted by the Anonimo Fiorentino at the margins of a single of Dante's verses – and in a substantially incongruous way, as noted – thus reduces in the end to a simple 'learned' citation, called up almost passively. Put otherwise, it does not delineate the conscious statement of a fundamental interpretive principle. In Petrarch, as already in Macrobius (*In Somnum Scipionis* I.2, §§ 17–21) and subsequently in Boccaccio, the figural language of the poets is above all an instrument to protect the truth from those who are not worthy to receive it. The Anonimo Fiorentino does not seem to share this idea. Or rather, he does not seem to draw from it the necessary consequences. Indeed, in the comment of the Anonimo Fiorentino there are lacking references to the so-to-speak esoteric nature of Dante's language. To the contrary: when at the beginning of his commentary the Anonimo Fiorentino writes that Dante decided to compose the *Commedia* in the vernacular so as to reach a wider and, from the political point of view, more influential audience, he seems to judge the poet's choice entirely positively.

Just as Guglielmo Maramauro, the Anonimo Fiorentino too receives the reflections of Petrarch and Boccaccio on poetry only in fragmentary forms. As compared to Maramauro, the Anonimo assimilates a good number of passages from the 'theoretician' Petrarch; but this notwithstanding, he does not demonstrate that he has succeeded in gathering them together into a unified idea. Or rather, he does not seem interested in doing this at all. There might be a variety of reasons for this. Before anything, it should be underlined that the Anonimo Fiorentino's commentary is, in many respects, a work strongly characterised by passivity. In point of fact, the Anonimo Fiorentino makes use of a large number of previous commentaries, which he often reiterates without modifying. His commentary on the *Paradiso*, for example, is so similar to that of Iacomo della Lana that the manuscript which transmits it – Florence, Biblioteca Riccardiana 1013 – can be considered no more than a translation in Tuscan of Iacomo's commentary.[36]

Given these facts, it is not surprising that the pieces he took from Petrarch's theoretical work remain essentially isolated from one another. But it is interesting to observe that each time the Anonimo Fiorentino attempts to sketch out a reflection on poetry and on language, he does so by citing the passages of Petrarch. This demonstrates that the authority of Petrarch as a theoretician of poetry was entirely consolidated by the end of the fourteenth century, since it extended even over a minor author like the Anonimo Fiorentino. There is also another element which ought to be emphasised here. In contrast to Boccaccio, the Anonimo Fiorentino does not perceive in Petrarch's ideas any clear threat to Dante's poetry, nor for poetry in the vernacular more generally. And even Guglielmo Maramauro, as we know, proved totally numb to the preoccupations which had tormented his master Boccaccio.

## The occasional prevalence of Petrarch, the vernacular poet, over Petrarch, the theoretician of poetry (and detractor of vernacular poetry)

In this context, something further can be said on the relation between Maramauro and the Anonimo Fiorentino on the one hand and Petrarch on the other. They are indeed the only of Dante's interpreters in the fourteenth century to cite certain Petrarchian texts in the vernacular in their comments. As I have written in the *Prologue*, mention of vernacular works by Petrarch in the commentaries on the *Commedia* of the late fourteenth century are extremely rare. After all, it was Petrarch himself who invited his readers to neglect his production in the vernacular: Petrarch stated several times (dishonestly, as we know) that he had dedicated himself to the vernacular only in the course of his youth – a time of life which is at its most unstable, since it is subjugated to irrational impulses and therefore is 'naturally' disposed to being described by a language which is in its turn unstable and mutable.

The fact that, in general, Dante's commentators consider Petrarch's Latin writings – his poetry, and above all his treatises – to be considerably more authoritative as compared to those in the vernacular can likely be interpreted as a sign of the reception which this aspect of Petrarch's intellectual self-portrait would receive.

Although they read and employ the vernacular work of Petrarch in their commentaries, Maramauro and the Anonimo Fiorentino do not constitute a real exception to this portrait. Indeed, both cite the *Rerum vulgarium fragmenta* (*Canzoniere*), but always selecting those passages that have nothing to do with the central theme of the book, namely, the love of the poet for Laura. Petrarch the vernacular poet of Maramauro and the Anonimo Fiorentino, in other words, *is not* a lyric poet – he is not a poet who treats of the passions, or rather who gives expression to the passions through his verses. He is instead a moral poet, or even a political poet.

Let us take a few examples. In the commentary on *Inf.* VIII.4, Maramauro cites a verse of sonnet 137 from the *Rerum vulgarium fragmenta*, establishing thereby a connection between the "high tower" of the infernal city of Dis, which, by Maramauro's judgement, represents arrogance, and the "haughty tower" of Petrarch's Babilonia-Avignon. Maramauro is probably citing from memory, given that he relays Petrarch's verse with an error.[37] For his part, the Anonimo Fiorentino cites the *Fragmenta* of Petrarch five times.[38] All the citations are concentrated on the comment on cantos IV–IX of the *Purgatorio*, and in none of these does he so much as touch upon the theme of love. The verses cited by Petrarch have moreover a moral significance: they are employed as wisdom maxims which serve to consolidate the teaching that can be extracted from the commented verses of the *Commedia*. It is important to note, however, that the moral judgement extracted by Petrarch sometimes does not perfectly fit the verses of Dante to which it is matched and thus ends up giving them different meaning.

One example will suffice to clarify this point. In canto IV of the *Purgatorio*, the soul of Belacqua, the exceedingly lazy musician of Florence, speaks ironically to Dante, saying (vv. 119–120): "Have you seen clearly how the sun drives his chariot over our left shoulder?".[39] Belacqua pokes fun at the scientific exactitude that Dante had exhibited just a little before, when, together with Virgil, he enlarged on an analysis of the movements of the sun in the two hemispheres (vv. 55–96). As Robert Hollander notes, "after having his actions described in ways that mark his physical laziness, Belacqua takes aim at Dante (and, guilty by association, Virgil)".[40] The Anonimo Fiorentino too comments these verses in the same way: "'What have you done, Dante? Have you studied the movements of the sun through and through? And what have you gained thereby?'. So says Belacqua, almost scolding the author". But then the Anonimo Fiorentino adds a citation from Petrarch which confers on this scene of the fourth canto of the *Purgatorio* a different and considerably less 'carefree' meaning: "Even Messer Francis [Petrarch], in one of his sonnets, speaks on this topic: 'Qual vagheçça di lauro, quale di mirto? Povera, ingnuda vai filosofia, dice la gente al vil guadagno intesa' etc.".[41]

The cited verses derive from sonnet 7 of the *Fragmenta*, *Gluttony and sleep and the pillows of idleness*, vv. 9–11: "What desire for the laurel is there? or for the myrtle? 'Philosophy, you go poor and naked!' says the mob, bent on low again".[42] Petrarch speaks, with evident disdain, to whomever neglects science in favour of economic profit: the ignorant "mob" deride philosophy because they consider it an activity which does not produce gain. Citing these verses of Petrarch, the Anonimo Fiorentino attributes a different moral profile to Belacqua than that which Dante wished to ascribe to him: in the context of canto IV of the *Purgatorio*, Dante's Belacqua does not represent that man who despises science, but he is simply a symbol – a deliberately silly and almost 'charming' symbol – of extreme laziness. Belacqua does not judge Dante's effort useless insofar as it is spent in philosophical speculation, but rather in terms of its exertion: to Belacqua's eyes, indeed, every exertion is useless – including evidently even that which is undertaken to obtain some advantage. This is demonstrated in what follows. Belacqua, though he is entirely aware that his punishment will conclude the moment he has reached the summit of the mount of Purgatory, does not seem to be desirous to undertake that climb (vv. 123–135).

Petrarch's citation, in other words, ends up modifying the meaning of Dante's text. The verses of sonnet 7 of the *Fragmenta* completely erase the comic implications of the episode and, beyond this, invite the reader to perceive in the sequence of the encounter between Dante and Belacqua a moral question different from that which is actually transmitted. Among these two consequences, the second appears to be certainly the more important. But the first, too, should not be underestimated. In Dante's *Commedia*, it is exceedingly rare that space is granted to the comic and, more generally, judgements on vicious behaviour seldom provide an occasion, however minor, for a benevolent condescension. (when Dante hears the words of Belacqua, he reacts with a smile: "His lazy movements and his brief words moved my lips to smile a little", *Purg.* IV.121–122). It is thus noteworthy that this rare 'infraction' – with its occasional and minimal vibration of ambiguity – is immediately corrected by the Anonimo Fiorentino; and it is more interesting still that it is corrected by recourse to Petrarch.

## Ambiguous episodes

All of the passages that we have examined so far permit multiple interpretations. Moreover, whenever one studies the ways in which different texts and authors interact with one another, it is rare that things appear without a certain character of ambiguity. And the picture grows more complicated when the authors under examination are commentators of the works of others, and above all when the commentators are 'minor' commentators, which is to say, incapable of expressing a strong and conscious idea regarding the text they are commenting.

Let us return to the quotations from the *Rerum vulgarium fragmenta* which we find in the Anonimo Fiorentino's commentary on the *Commedia*. On the one hand, as I have said, the Anonimo Fiorentino selects only passages from Petrarch's production in the vernacular in which there is no reference to the theme of love, and this could be read as a sign of acknowledgement on the part of the Anonimo Fiorentino of the clear-cut censorship that the 'mature' Petrarch set upon his own previous works. But, on the other hand, are we certain that the Anonimo Fiorentino was aware of Petrarch's self-censorship? In truth, we are not certain of it.

The citations from the *Fragmenta* in the commentary of the Anonimo Fiorentino might indeed have a completely different meaning. We have stated that the Anonimo Fiorentino never gives sign of considering poetry in the vernacular inferior to poetry in Latin; in consequence, it is not surprising that he uses Petrarch's *Fragmenta* in his commentary. From a certain point of view, this observation already offers us an important indication on the relation that the Anonimo Fiorentino established with the poetical rules elaborated and promoted by Petrarch. To all available evidence, the Anonimo Fiorentino did not perceive Petrarch's aversion toward vernacular poetry; and even if he did perceive it, he did not take it into account. Indeed, the fact that Petrarch's vernacular verses are used to explain Dante could even be read as the recognition of Dante's superiority over Petrarch: in the Anonimo Fiorentino's commentary, it is indeed Petrarch who 'lends' his own verses toward a better comprehension of the *Commedia*. In addition, the fact that the Anonimo Fiorentino, in his quotations from the *Fragmenta*, selects only passages lacking any reference to the theme of love could also be understood in terms other than those that we have assumed up to now: it may be less the effect of an acknowledgement of the poetic self-portrait elaborated by the 'mature' Petrarch than the result of a voluntary adaptation of Petrarch's work to the themes treated in the *Commedia*. This second hypothesis seems to be more probable. And yet, as we have observed, the 'service' rendered to Dante by Petrarch in the commentary of the Anonimo Fiorentino is not without its consequences.

In this respect, we must dedicate some space to discussing an episode that presents a similar ambiguity – but a deeper one yet. Already by the end of the fourteenth century, or in the first years of the following century, as has been established,[43] some manuscripts began to circulate in which the *Commedia* of Dante was placed side-by-side with a commentary written in the vernacular that was explicitly attributed to Petrarch. In this way Petrarch, just like Boccaccio, becomes a commentator of Dante. On the last page of the manuscript Barberiniano Latino 4116 of the Biblioteca Apostolica Vaticana, we read this surprising *explicit* (f. 186*ra*):

> Here concludes the exposition on the *Commedia* of Dante Alighieri of Florence, composed by the expert theologian and *magister* Francis Petrarch of Florence, the only poet in the world crowned with the poetic laurels.[44]

The same words occurred in the *explicit* of two other manuscripts: the manuscript Gaddi 90 sup. 120 of the Biblioteca Laurenziana of Florence (early fifteenth century) and the manuscript Campori App. 64 of the Biblioteca Estense e Universitaria of Modena (also early fifteen century). All three of these manuscripts transmit, beyond the text of the *Commedia*, one and the same commentary: a commentary written in the vernacular, structured as a continuous exposition of Dante's entire poem, from the first verse of the *Inferno* to the last verse of the *Paradiso*. Naturally, and counter the claims in the *explicit* of the three manuscripts, the true author of this commentary is not Petrarch. The true author is Iacomo della Lana, an interpreter of Dante from Bologna; we owe to him one of the first commentaries on the *Commedia* known to us, written between 1324 and 1328, which is to say, just a few years after Dante's death.[45]

The attribution of the authorship of the commentary by Iacomo della Lana to Petrarch, it is needless to say, is bizarre. How can we interpret it? Here, too, having no information about who is responsible for this operation – and therefore no effective knowledge of his 'motives' – it is impossible to give a definitive answer to this question; we can only formulate a few conjectures. Let us begin from what we know with certainty, and let us try to examine these facts with attention. In the *explicit* that I have transcribed and translated above, various titles are attributed to Petrarch. Consider the last: Petrarch is defined as the "only poet in the world crowned with the poetic laurels". This, too, is false. Or rather: it is true that Petrarch was crowned poet laureate, but it is not at all true that he was the only one in the world to have obtained this honour. In the medieval period alone, Albertino Mussato should also be recalled here; he was crowned as the poet laureate and historian in Padua in 1315. And some years after the crowning of Petrarch (1342), Zanobi da Strada also obtained the same recognition: this happened in 1355, a few decades before the epoch in which the manuscript indicating Petrarch as the only one to have deserved this title was written.

The formula "the only poet in the world crowned with the poetic laurels" thus contains an exaggeration, on the basis of which Petrarch appears to be the greatest poet of his time – or maybe even the greatest poet of all times. This is the first fact which must be highlighted. Based on what we read in the *explicit* of the three manuscripts, the greatest poet in the world set himself to writing a commentary on Dante's *Commedia*. Luca Carlo Rossi has acutely observed that if the commentary "is made to play the part of a servant", as Dante himself wrote in the *Convivio*, then Petrarch certainly becomes Dante's "servant": Petrarch

> acquiesces to making himself the servant of Dante's poem and, more-over, submits to Dante's decision to write in the vernacular; given that the poet laureate bent to so humble a duty, Dante must be worthy of the tribute, and thus must be the supreme poet.[46]

In light of this fact, the attribution of Iacomo della Lana's commentary to Petrarch almost has the feeling of mockery. Nor is this an isolated event. At least one other commentary on Dante is attributed to Petrarch, it too in the vernacular: this was an introduction, or rather a prologue, on the *Commedia* transmitted through all of eight manuscripts. In two of these manuscripts, the authorship of the prologue is explicitly attributed to Petrarch: namely, the manuscript 1036 of the Biblioteca Riccardiana of Florence and the manu-script once known as 'Phillipps 247', today preserved in New York in the private library of H. P. Kraus. Both of these manuscripts date back to the beginning of the fifteenth century.[47] We are thus still in the period upon which we have so far turned our attention: the last years of the fourteenth century, and the very first of the fifteenth century, a phase still prior to the elaboration of what would afterwards be defined as the canon of the *Tre Corone*.

This prologue is generally identified by a title which is itself already very significant, especially in light of what we read in the *explicit* of the three manuscripts that attributed Iacomo della Lana's commentary to Petrarch. The title of the prologue, taken from its first words, is *Dante poeta sovrano* (*Dante, Sovereign Poet*). Let us read the first lines, transcribing (and trans-lating) them from the version preserved in manuscript 1036 of the Biblioteca Riccardiana of Florence, one of the two documents that explicitly attribute this text to Petrarch (f. 1v):

> Dante, sovereign poet, crown and glory of the vernacular, Florentine by birth but not by his mores, . . . great example and model of culture and nobility of spirit, expert in every field of knowledge, wrote this marvel-lous work, to which he gave a title in the Greek tongue: *Commedia*.[48]

These words do not seem to contrast altogether with the judgement on Dante expressed by the 'true' Petrarch. In the *Fam.* XX.15, Petrarch admits without hesitation that Dante was the greatest among the poets in the vernacular (§ 13): "to whom [i.e. to Dante] I would readily grant the palm for vernacular eloquence"; and he repeats the same judgement some years after in the *Sen.* V.2, where he defines Dante "the master of our vernacular literature" (§ 30). Yet the title 'sovereign' seems to imply that the praise expressed in the prologue is not limited to the field of the vernacular poetry alone: Dante seems to qualify as the 'sovereign' of all poets, vernacular and Latin alike.

This is confirmed by what follows. Before we read any further passages of this document, however, I still must state that the words I have transcribed, as those which I will shortly quote, have a known author, and he is not, as goes without saying, Petrarch: the author is in fact Guido da Pisa, who around middle of the 1330s wrote a commentary on the *Inferno*, along with other important interpretive texts on Dante's poem. The prologue *Dante poeta sovrano* is in fact, for the most part, the translation into vernacular of the preface of the *Expositiones* on the *Inferno* by Guido da Pisa.[49] The expression "poeta sovrano" is not contained in the preface of the *Expositiones* but belongs nonetheless to Guido da Pisa, who uses it in the introductory verses of his *Declaratio super "Comediam" Dantis* (vv. 3–6): "Dante, sovereign poet | who showed the way to access every virtue | following a path both divine and human".[50] As can be seen, the expression "poeta sovrano" is contained in these verses, but not the image of the "corona". It is interesting that this image is used in relation to Dante's excellence in vernacular poetry. The formula "corona et gloria della lingua latina" – where "Latin tongue" obviously means the vernacular, as in *Inf.* XXVII.33 – indeed anticipates by several decades that used by Giovanni Gherardi in his *Paradiso degli Alberti*, where Dante, Petrarch and Boccaccio are indicated as the "tre corone fiorentine" that have ennobled their "edioma materno", their mother tongue, the vernacular.[51] Beginning with Giovanni Gherardi, the image of the 'tre corone' was destined to attain an extraordinary fortune, as we well know.

The passage that I have transcribed here concludes on the question of the poem's title, *Commedia*. Following the proem *Dante poeta sovrano*, just as in the proem of Guido da Pisa's *Expositiones*, it is precisely this aspect of Dante's work to be analysed – namely, the meaning of its title. Guido da Pisa believes that the title of the poem is reductive, given that it recalls a subject and a style that, in and of themselves, in no way exhaust the thematic and rhetorical richness of the *Commedia*. After an in-depth *excursus* on different styles of poetry – lyrical, satirical, tragic, comic – Guido arrives at this conclusion: in the *Commedia*, Dante succeeded in reuniting all these genres and styles, fulfilling all their possibilities and thus giving life to a poem that has no precedent in the history of literature. I quote a passage of the prologue of the *Expositiones*, in English translation:

> Dante should not be called just a comic poet on account of having written the *Commedia*.[52] Dante should also be called a lyric poet for the variety of his verses and for the sweet sound that they propagate; and he should be called a satirical poet, for the fact that in his poem he harshly denounces the vices and exalts the virtues; and he should also be called a tragic poet, because he recounts memorable episodes whose protagonists are high-ranking people.[53]

This passage is also related by the author of the prologue *Dante poeta sovrano*. I transcribe below the original version, followed by its translation (manuscript Ricc. 1036, f. 2r – v):

> Ma questo magnificho et excelso poeta è non solamente poeta chomico, per la materia della quale tracta, ma etiandio poeta liricho per le diverse rime che ei fece, che non fu huomo che sì dolcemente parlasse et trovasse chome fecie elli. Fu etiandio questo poeta satiro, per le reprentioni che fecie de' vitii et per le chomendationi che fece delle virtudi. Fu etiandio sommo tragedo, per lo tractare che fe' de' grandi et memorabili fatti delli antichi et anche moderni principi et signori.

> But this magnificent and sublime poet is not only a comic poet: he demonstrates this with the subject which he treats in his work. He is also a lyric poet for the variety of his verses and the rhymes that he has composed: there was no one that was able to match him in the sweetness of his verses. And he was also a satirical poet, because in his work he condemns the vices and praises the virtues. And he was also an excellent tragic poet, because he tells about great memorable facts that have as their protagonists princes and kings, both from ancient and modern times.

The similarities between this passage and its source are evident. The translator reproduces Guido da Pisa's argument without changing it. However, he accentuates the praise of Dante. He adds that no poet has ever composed verses as beautiful as those composed by Dante. And, in the last sentence, he clarifies that the memorable stories collected by Dante in the *Commedia* involve both the past and the present. This is an interesting clarification, as we will see in the final chapter of this book.

## Another mystery: an unknown letter of Petrarch, Francesco da Buti and the prologue *Dante poeta sovrano*

It would be well to return to the point at which we began. Someone we do not know, at an unspecified moment – but located in any case somewhere between the end of the fourteenth and the beginning of the fifteenth centuries – attributed the words that we have just read to Petrarch. According to this attribution, Petrarch celebrated Dante not only as the "crown" of the vernacular language, but also as the greatest poet of all time: nobody before Dante had succeeded in combining all genres and all styles within a single work; that is why Dante can be considered "poeta sovrano". In addition to the recognition of the absolute superiority of Dante over any other poet, it is important also to highlight the argument on which this recognition is founded. Dante as poet reprised and reunited in one single work all the poetical precedent experiences, ancient and modern, Latin and vernacular: the *Commedia*, in other words, includes within itself, and thus exhausts, all the possibilities of literary creation. Furthermore, Dante is celebrated as the heir to an uninterrupted tradition: this means that in the eyes of Guido da Pisa – and those who have translated his words – there is no rupture between the ancient literature and the modern, between poetry in Latin and in the vernacular. In this way, the idea that the choice of the vernacular was for Dante a makeshift, following several initial attempts in Latin, is radically denied.[54] As in the case of the attribution of Iacomo della Lana's commentary to Petrarch, here too it seems we perceive the will to correct Petrarch's true judgement on Dante by acting directly on the criteria that lay behind that judgement.

It is possible to add another fact to the those we have gathered up to now, this one in its turn quite curious. At the beginning of this chapter, I quoted another of the *Commedia*'s late fourteenth century commentators, who was certainly exposed to the influence of both Boccaccio and Petrarch: Francesco da Buti, who wrote his commentary between 1390 and 1396 after having given a public lecture on the *Commedia* in Pisa in 1385.[55] In Francesco da Buti's commentary, there are numerous contacts with Boccaccio's *Esposizioni*, and they take on a noteworthy importance. Compared to the Anonimo Fiorentino, Francesco da Buti is more faithful in his use of Boccaccio's commentary. For example, he recovers Boccaccio's systematic subdivision between a literal interpretation and an allegoric interpretation of Dante's verses, and he goes so far as to suppose that some readers are interested exclusively in the allegoric meaning of the poem and not in the literal one. Indeed, Francesco da Buti writes that the "studiosi", which is to say 'wise men', "prefer a brief exposition of the text, and feel intellectually satisfied only when the allegoric meaning has been illustrated to them".[56]

In the light of this passage, we also perceive that Francesco da Buti does not consider the vernacular unsuitable for a cultivated public – quite the contrary. This fact is meaningful, because, in contrast to the commentators cited up to now, Francesco da Buti was also a great interpreter of the Latin classics – Plautus, Terence, Statius, Persius, and Horace[57] – as well as the author of a manual of Latin grammar which, as Robert Black has written, was "the most widely circulated and important secondary grammar manual" of Italy at that time.[58] Evidently, for Francesco da Buti, it is not the language which selects the public but rather the depth of the topic covered and the way in which it is treated – in particular, an allegorical, 'ciphered' approach, which is not immediately intelligible without the right key to access it.

And Petrarch? Francesco da Buti mentions him only once, but in an extremely interesting context, especially if we put it in relation with what we have already read in the prologue *Dante poeta sovrano*. In truth, Francesco da Buti's reference to Petrarch is rather surprising in itself. He cites a letter by Petrarch which we do not know: perhaps this letter has not been preserved, or perhaps it has yet to be discovered.[59] In this unknown letter, Petrarch evidently criticises Dante for having entitled his poem *Commedia*. Already in the proem of his commentary, Francesco da Buti mentioned the fact that the title *Commedia* might seem incongruous as compared to the matter and the style of the poem, but he did not linger on the question: he referred his readers to the comprehensive treatment of this problem found in the pages dedicated to this subject by Boccaccio in his *Esposizioni*.[60] Commenting on the first verses of canto XXI of the *Inferno*, and in particular v. 2 ("other things that *my comedy* does not record"), Francesco da Buti returns to the issue, writing:

> Some might express a doubt: should this poem to be indicated with the title of *Commedia* or not? Given that Dante decided to entitle his work in this way, we must accept his decision and speak of it using this title. Petrarch, in a letter that begins with the words *Ne te laudasse poeniteat* etc., discusses this problem, writing: 'Nec cur *Comediam* vocet video' ('I do not see for what reason he entitled his poem *Commedia*').[61]

As mentioned, the letter quoted by Francesco da Buti is unknown. We do not even know who the addressee of Petrarch's letter was. Some think that the letter might have been addressed to Boccaccio: it could therefore be another document in the dialogue between Petrarch and Boccaccio on Dante – a different document, however, from the *Fam.* XXI.15, where Petrarch makes no polemic references to the title of the *Commedia*.[62] As a matter of fact, writing to Petrarch in 1367 (*Ep.* XV), Boccaccio informs him of having never received several letters that Petrarch had sent to him, among which was one dedicated specifically to Dante's work.[63] Might it be precisely this the letter which somehow fell – we know not how – into the hands of Francesco da Buti?

Be that as it may, the point that I wish to highlight is another. There are indeed two different issues in this passage which are, however, strictly bound to one another. The first one is the more obvious: in contrast with the commentators on whom we have focused in the previous pages – Guglielmo Maramauro and the Anonimo Fiorentino – Francesco da Buti demonstrates that he was directly aware of the criticisms that Petrarch addressed to Dante's work. But the criticisms to which Francesco da Buti refers are not the ones that we would expect: they do not concern the language of the *Commedia*, that vernacular against which Petrarch elsewhere expressed so much contempt, but rather its title. Precisely this element permits us to identify a connection between the reports of Francesco da Buti and the prologue *Dante poeta sovrano*. Indeed, the false-Petrarch who appropriates to himself Guido da Pisa's words also believes that the title that Dante has given to his poem is partially inappropriate: "But this magnificent and sublime poet is not only a comic poet: he demonstrates this with the subject which he treats in his work" (manuscript Ricc. 1036, f. 2r). However, in the context of that prologue, the fact that the title *Commedia* is not altogether appropriate provides an opportunity to sing Dante's praises. And this is not any ordinary praise but the greatest praise conceivable, as we have observed earlier: Dante is celebrated as the man who has surpassed every other poet, ancient and modern, by practising in an excellent way all the genres of the poetry in a single work. If Petrarch, in a letter which is today unknown to us, truly criticised Dante for having entitled his poem *Commedia*, the anonymous author that attributed the prologue *Dante poeta sovrano* to Petrarch has reversed the meaning of that critique, transforming it into open acclaim. We do not know, obviously, if this was done deliberately. But certainly the effect is evident, and it is remarkable.

There is more still. I have said that the prologue *Dante poeta sovrano* begins with the celebration of Dante as the "crown and glory of the vernacular". The true Petrarch, as we know, also considered Dante the greatest of the vernacular poets. But from the perspective of Petrarch, such excellence is nothing if not limitation. Let us read another passage of the *Fam.* XXI.15 (§§ 24–25):

I have at times said only one thing to those who wished to know my exact thoughts: his [i.e. Dante's] style was unequal, for he rises to nobler and loftier heights in the vernacular than in Latin poetry or prose. Not even you will deny this, nor does it redound to anything but his praise and glory in the minds of sensible judges. Forgetting the present age inasmuch as eloquence has long since vanished and been buried, and speaking only of the age when it flourished, who, I ask, excelled in all its branches? Read Seneca's *Declamationes*: it is not conceded to Cicero or to Virgil, to Sallust or to Plato. Who would aspire to praises denied such great geniuses? It suffices to have excelled in one genre.

If we read this page in the light of what is said in the prologue *Dante poeta sovrano*, we will once more have the impression that we find ourselves standing before a deliberate reversal. According to Petrarch, the excellence of Dante in the vernacular poetry corresponds to excellence "in one genre". In *Dante poeta sovrano*, meanwhile, the judgement on Dante's excellence as a vernacular poet carries us spontaneously toward a contrary conclusion: Dante, "crown and glory of the vernacular", excels in every poetical genre and excels in all poetical genres at once. The question that Petrarch raises at the end of the passage extracted from the *Fam.* XXI.15 thus finds, in the prologue *Dante poeta sovrano*, a clear and definitive answer: "Who would aspire to praises denied such great geniuses?" – Dante, no doubt.

## Notes

1  The contents of Benvenuto's letter are inferred, as one might imagine, directly from Petrarch's answer. See what L. C. Rossi writes in this regard: *Studi su Benvenuto da Imola* (Florence: SISMEL Edizioni del Galluzzo, 2016), 166–169.

2  See G. Maramauro, *Expositione sopra l'* *"Inferno"* *di Dante Alligieri*, ed. by P. G. Pisoni and S. Bellomo (Padua: Antenore, 1998), 82.

3  See Pisoni-Bellomo, 'Introduzione', in Maramauro, *Expositione*, 5–6 and 23; see also 'Guglielmo Maramauro', in *Censimento dei commenti danteschi*, ed. by E. Malato and A. Mazzucchi, vol. 1, *I commenti di tradizione manoscritta (fino al 1428)* (Rome: Salerno, 2011), tome 1, 263.

4  There are also some (for instance Rossi, *Studi su Benvenuto da Imola*, 224) who believe that Maramauro was able to attend Boccaccio's lessons on the *Commedia* and that the convergence between Maramauro's commentary and Boccaccio's *Esposizioni* are therefore explicable as emerging from the notes that the former had taken while listening to the latter commenting Dante. According to this view, however, Maramauro must have finished his commentary after October 1373, and this seems irreconcilable with what Maramauro himself claims: see *Prologo*, §§ 10–11 (Maramauro, *Expositione*, 81). I upheld a similar hypothesis to Rossi's in L. Fiorentini, 'Archaeology of the *Tre Corone*', *Dante Studies* 136 (2018), 2. Today, however, I am of a different mind. Indeed, it seems strange to me that Maramauro never refers in his commentary to the public lectures on the *Commedia* given by Boccaccio.

5  See, for example, Benvenuto da Imola, *Comentum super Dantis Aldigherij* *"Comoediam"*, ed. by G. F. Lacaita, 5 tomes (Florence: Barbera, 1887), tome 3, 171 (*ad Purg.* VI 16–18).

6  For an initial glance at the ensemble of Boccaccian works used by Benvenuto in his commentary on the *Commedia*, see Rossi, *Studi su Benvenuto da Imola*,

203–270, and L. Fiorentini, *Per Benvenuto da Imola* (Bologna: il Mulino, 2016), 167–173, 475–533, etc.

7　See once more the 'Introduzione' by Pisoni-Bellomo in Maramauro, *Expositione*, 31.

8　For a preliminary framework on these three commentators, see the entries 'Filippo Villani', 'Anonimo Fiorentino' and 'Francesco da Buti', in *Censimento dei commenti danteschi*, tome 1 187–191 (by B. Basile), 36–42 (by F. Geymonat) and 192–218 (by F. Franceschini).

9　For a more detailed narration of Maramauro's life, see the 'Introduzione' by Pisoni-Bellomo in Maramauro, *Expositione*, 3–22.

10　See L. C. Rossi, 'Petrarca dantista involontario', *Studi petrarcheschi* 5 (1988), 312.

11　Here again I employ the translation of the *Fam.* XXI.15 by Aldo S. Bernardo: see F. Petrarca, *Letters on Familiar Matters, Rerum familiarum libri XVI–XXIV*, trans. by A. S. Bernardo (Baltimore-London: The Johns Hopkins University Press, 1985), 202–207.

12　The passage is taken from *Sen.* XV.4, §§ 1–2, which I cite from the translation of Aldo S. Bernardo, Saul Levin and Reta A. Bernardo: F. Petrarch, *Letters of Old Age (Rerum senilium libri)*, vol. 2, *Books X–XVIII* (New York: Italica Press, 2005), 569–750.

13　See L. C. Rossi, 'Presenze di Petrarca in commenti danteschi fra Tre e Quattrocento', *Aevum* 70/3 (1996), 443–445.

14　Maramauro, *Expositione*, 84.

15　I use the translation of the *Commedia* by Robert M. Durling: see *The Divine Comedy of Dante Alighieri*, I, *Inferno*, ed. and trans. by R. M. Durling, introduction and notes by R. L. Martinez and R. M. Durling (New York-Oxford: Oxford University Press, 1996).

16　See B. Croce, *The poetry of Dante*, trans. by D. Ainslie (London: George Allen & Unwin, 1922), 102–103.

17　See Maramauro, *Expositione*, 207.

18　I quote the *Collatio laureationis* from C. Godi, 'La *Collatio laureationis* del Petrarca nelle due redazioni', *Studi petrarcheschi* 5 (1988), 1–58. The translation is mine.

19　As in Chapter I, I employ here the translation of Aldo S. Bernardo: see F. Petrarca, *Letters on Familiar Matters, Rerum familiarum libri IX–XVI*, trans. by A. S. Bernardo (Baltimore-London: The Johns Hopkins University Press, 1982), 69–75.

20　I employ as always the translation of M. Papio, *Boccaccio's "Expositions" on Dante's "Comedy"*, trans. by M. Papio (Toronto-Buffalo-London: University of Toronto Press, 2009).

21　G. Boccaccio, *Esposizioni sopra la "Comedia"*, ed. by G. Padoan (Milan: Mondadori, 1965), 480.

22　See *Commento alla "Divina Commedia" d'Anonimo Fiorentino del secolo XIV*, ed. by P. Fanfani, 3 tomes (Bologna: Romagnoli, 1866–1874).

23　See Geymonat, 'Anonimo Fiorentino', 36 (with bibliography).

24　See S. Bellomo, *Dizionario dei commentatori danteschi* (Florence: Olschki, 2004), 99, and Geymonat, 'Anonimo Fiorentino', 40–41.

25　See Rossi, 'Presenze di Petrarca', 463–468, and F. Geymonat, 'Fonti non esegetiche nel commento alla *Commedia* dell'Anonimo Fiorentino', *Rivista di studi danteschi* 2 (2002), 334–377.

26  *Commento d'Anonimo Fiorentino*, tome 1, 6–7.
27  *Commento d'Anonimo Fiorentino*, tome 2, 14. The other quotation of the *Fam.* X.4, contained in the comment to *Purg.* XXI.95, is not dissimilar from a conceptual point of view: see Geymonat, 'Fonti non esegetiche', 371–372.
28  *Commento d'Anonimo Fiorentino*, tome 1, 20–21.
29  See Geymonat, 'Fonti non esegetiche', 336–365.
30  About these verses, see among others T. Barolini, *Dante's Poets* (Princeton, NJ: Princeton University Press, 1984), 223–226.
31  All passages of the original version of Dante's poem are taken from the edition by Giorgio Inglese: D. Alighieri, *Commedia*, edition and commentary by G. Inglese, 3 vols. (Rome: Carocci, 2016).
32  *Commento d'Anonimo Fiorentino*, tome 1, 532.
33  This is Rossi's opinion: see 'Presenze di Petrarca', 464–465.
34  This on the other hand is what Geymonat holds: see 'Fonti non esegetiche', 374.
35  As in the first chapter, I cite the translation by David Marsh: see F. Petrarch, *Invectives*, ed. and trans. by D. Marsh (Cambridge, MA-London, England: The I Tatti Renaissance Library-Harvard University Press, 2003).
36  See Geymonat, 'Anonimo Fiorentino', 36.
37  See the note by Pisoni-Bellomo in Maramauro, *Expositione*, 192, and Rossi, 'Presenze di Petrarca', 444–445.
38  See Geymonat, 'Fonti non esegetiche', 360–365.
39  I again employ the translation of Robert M. Durling: see here *The Divine Comedy of Dante Alighieri*, II, *Purgatorio*, ed. and trans. by R. M. Durling, introduction and notes by R. L. Martinez and R. M. Durling (New York-Oxford: Oxford University Press, 2003).
40  D. Alighieri, *Purgatorio*, trans. by J. Hollander and R. Hollander, introduction and notes by R. Hollander (New York: Anchor Books, 2004).
41  *Commento d'Anonimo Fiorentino*, tome 2, 74.
42  I employ the translation of Robert M. Durling: see *Petrarch's Lyric Poems*, trans. and ed. by R. M. Durling (Cambridge, MA-London, England: Harvard University Press, 1976).
43  See L. C. Rossi, 'Petrarca dantista involontario', 305–306, and Bellomo, *Dizionario dei commentatori danteschi*, 375–377.
44  Here follows the original version, transcribed from the manuscript Barb. Lat. 4116, f. 186*ra*: "Explicit glosa sive expositio super *Comediam* Dantis Allegherii de Florentia composita per discretum theologum magistrum dominum Franciscum de Petracchis de Florentia, nec non unicum poetam mundi lauree corone corone [*sic*] coronatum".
45  See M. Volpi, 'Iacomo della Lana', in *Censimento dei commenti danteschi*, tome 1, 294–295.
46  Rossi, 'Petrarca dantista involontario', 308. Translation is mine.
47  See F. Franceschini, '*Dante poeta sovrano* and the *Codex altonensis*', in *Esercizi di lettura per Marco Santagata*, ed. by A. Andreoni, C. Giunta and M. Tavoni (Bologna: il Mulino, 2017), 82–83, n. 3.
48  The translation is mine. For the original version, see the manuscript Ricc. 1036, f. 1*v*. In the same manuscript, these words are preceded by a heading in which we read: "Prologue to the first *cantica* of the *Commedia* of Dante Alighieri, poet of Florence, written by Messer Francesco Petrarca, poet of Florence" ("Prolagho sopra la prima chanticha della *Chomedia* di Dante Alleghieri, poeta cittadino fiorentino, fatto per messer Francescho Petrarcha, poeta fiorentino").

49 The first to identify the prologue *Dante poeta sovrano* as a vernacular translation of Guido da Pisa was P. Colomb de Batines, *Bibliografia dantesca*, 2 tomes (Prato: Tip. Aldina, 1845–1846), tome 2, 300–301.

50 Guido da Pisa, *Expositiones et glose, Declaratio super "Comediam" Dantis*, ed. by M. Rinaldi and P. Locatin, 2 tomes (Rome: Salerno, 2013), tome 2, 985.

51 Giovanni Gherardi da Prato, *Il Paradiso degli Alberti*, ed. by A. Lanza (Rome: Salerno, 1975), 3–4. See the *Prologue* of this book.

52 According to Guido da Pisa (and others before him), the subject of the *Commedia* is 'comic' because it has a negative beginning (Hell) and a positive end (Paradise). The title of Dante's poem is explained in this way also in the *Epistle to Cangrande della Scala* (§ 29), whose author, according to some scholars, is Dante himself.

53 Guido da Pisa, *Expositiones et glose*, tome 1, 244–245.

54 See Franceschini, '*Dante, poeta sovrano*', 84.

55 See F. Franceschini, 'Francesco da Buti', in *Censimento dei commenti danteschi*, tome 1, 198–199.

56 Francesco da Buti, *Commento sopra la "Divina Commedia" di Dante Allighieri*, ed. by C. Giannini, 3 tomes (Pisa: Fratelli Nistri, 1858–1862), tome 1, 15.

57 See Franceschini, 'Francesco da Buti', 195.

58 R. Black, *Humanism and Education in Medieval and Renaissance Italy* (Cambridge: Cambridge University Press, 2001), 98–99.

59 See Rossi, 'Presenze di Petrarca', 462–463, and C. Paolazzi, 'Petrarca, Boccaccio e il *Trattatello in laude di Dante*', in *Dante e la "Comedia" nel Trecento* (Milan: Vita e Pensiero, 1989), 217–220.

60 See Francesco da Buti, *Commento*, tome 1, 7.

61 Francesco da Buti, *Commento*, tome 1, 543.

62 See Rossi, 'Presenze di Petrarca', 462.

63 See G. Boccaccio, *Tutte le opere*, vol. V/1, ed. by V. Branca *et alii* (Milan: Mondadori, 1992), 640.

# 3 Against Petrarch, theoretician of poetry

## Benvenuto da Imola

### The discovery of an already-existing canon

The portrait drawn up to this point presents various ambiguities but at the same time offers us fundamental information: at the end of the fourteenth century, it was not possible to undertake a commentary on Dante without encountering Petrarch and Boccaccio along the way. From this point of view, studying the reception of Dante at the end of the fourteenth century therefore means studying as well the earliest reception of Petrarch and Boccaccio, of their works and their thought. However, in the commentaries that we have analysed in the preceding chapters, the ways that Petrarch and Boccaccio exercise their influence on the interpretation of Dante appear, in most cases, varied and uncertain. Sometimes their presence is quite visible, at other times it is rather tenuous and indirect; and other times still, as in the case of the prologue *Dante poeta sovrano*, it is founded on evident mystifications, we know not whether caused by ingenuity or, rather, by a deliberate desire to correct the judgement of one of the members of the 'triad' on the work of another member. But there is also another fact which it is important to highlight here. Those Dantean commentators so far cited never once dwell on Petrarch and Boccaccio as such, assessing, for example, the points of continuity standing between their works on the one hand and Dante's poem on the other, or even expressing an explicit judgement on them. The commentators that we have examined make use of Petrarch and Boccaccio essentially to shed light on the *Commedia*: they use them as exegetic sources, so to speak. Not even Boccaccio himself is altogether an exception, given that, for reasons which are easy enough to comprehend, he never dares to compare himself to Dante or to Petrarch, neither in the *Trattatello* nor in the *Esposizioni*. Boccaccio compares Dante and Petrarch to one another and goes to great lengths to emphasise that there is a line of continuity between the two.[1] But in so doing, he systematically avoids any reference to himself.

If we pause on the texts that we have read up to this point, therefore, we can come to a partial conclusion. Starting from the 1370s, it is common to find the names of Petrarch and Boccaccio in the commentaries on Dante's *Commedia*. But the idea that the three poets constitute a cohesive group does not seem yet to have taken form. There is just the bare fact itself, so to speak, without any consciousness of that fact, without any conceptual re-elaboration of it.

Of course, this should not surprise us. The texts that we are studying are commentaries on Dante's poem, not essays of literary criticism. And nonetheless, there is an exception which seems to confer a completely different meaning to the story that I have attempted to narrate up to now. There is in fact one Dante commentator at the end of the fourteenth century who did not limit himself to citing, every so often, some passage or other of Petrarch and Boccaccio but who frequently reflects at length on these two authors, on their works and, above all, on their relationship to Dante; and he explicitly invites his readers to consider Dante, Petrarch and Boccaccio as the three great 'modern' poets, that is as models to whom every other author should make reference. If that canon which would subsequently be known as the canon of the *Tre Corone* has a precise birthday, it can probably be identified with the activity of this commentator, which is to say between the halfway point of the 1370s and the first half of the 1380s. He is placed therefore in the first part of the chronological period that we have considered: immediately after Guglielmo Maramauro and a bit before Francesco da Buti, the Anonimo Fiorentino and Filippo Villani. His name is Benvenuto da Imola, and it is to his commentary that I will dedicate my attention from here to the end of this book.

We know little about Benvenuto's life. He was born in Imola somewhere around the 1330s. About 1364 he composed his first work, the *Romuleon*, a synthesis of Roman history compiled in Latin, as would be the remainder of his works. In 1365, he went to Avignon in the office of ambassador on behalf of Imola to seek the aid of Pope Urban V against the government of the Alidosi, the city's rulers. His embassy was unsuccessful: the Alidosi became imperial vicars, and Benvenuto, like Dante, was exiled forever from his hometown. He moved then to Bologna, where, until 1375, he held courses on Dante's *Commedia* and on Valerius Maximus's *Memorable deeds and sayings*. In 1375, he was forced to quickly abandon Bologna – we do not know why. He reached Ferrara, where he resided, under the protection of Niccolò II d'Este, until the end of his life. In Ferrara, Benvenuto held a second course on the *Commedia* (winter of 1375–1376) and worked on the definitive edition of his Dante commentary, which was completed probably around 1383 but never definitively revised. In Ferrara, Benvenuto also commented Virgil (the *Bucolics* and the *Georgics*), Lucan, and

Petrarch (*Bucolicum carmen*); he also revised his commentary on Valerius Maximus and composed another work of historical synthesis, the *Libellus Augustalis*. He died, in all likelihood, in 1388.[2]

This brief biographical note permits us to highlight several interesting elements. Like Francesco da Buti, Benvenuto too dedicated himself to the study and the interpretation as much of modern literature as of ancient literature. But his interest in modern literature was not limited only to texts in the vernacular, which is to say, the Dante of the *Commedia*: Benvenuto has left us also a commentary on Petrarch's Latin poetry, the *Bucolicum carmen*. We should also underline the focus that Benvenuto da Imola put on ancient history. Indeed, he made his debut as a writer by publishing a compendium of Roman history, from the destruction of Troy to Diocletian: the *Romuleon*, which had an extraordinary diffusion and was translated various times into the vernacular, in both Italian and French; and he closed his career with another historiographical work, the *Libellus Augustalis*. But Benvenuto was moved by this special attention for ancient history also in his work as an interpreter of the classics, as his comments on Valerius Maximus and Lucan demonstrate. Naturally, such an interest in historical narration must have had a considerable weight as well on the interpretation of Dante which Benvenuto produced and also on the relation of Benvenuto to Petrarch and Boccaccio's oeuvre, as we shall see.

The better part of Benvenuto's works are still unpublished. I will cite therefore a number of passages from his 'minor' commentaries – and in particular, from his commentaries on Virgil and Petrarch – taking them directly from the manuscripts (in this case, the manuscripts 109 from the Biblioteca Statale of Cremona, for Virgil, and Lat. 8700 from the Bibliothèque Nationale de France, for Petrarch).[3] Of the three drafts of Benvenuto's commentary on the *Commedia*, only the first, that is the *recollectae* of the course held in Bologna in 1375, has been recently published in a reliable critical edition.[4] The *recollectae* of the second course held in Ferrara in the winter of 1375–1376 are totally unpublished, for which reason I will directly cite the principal manuscript that transmits them, the codex Ashburnham 839 of the Biblioteca Medicea Laurenziana of Florence. The definitive edition, meanwhile, can still be read in the version published by Giacomo Lacaita in 1887, also available on the website of the *Dartmouth Dante Project*.[5]

Benvenuto personally knew and frequented both Boccaccio and Petrarch. He was friends with the former: this is demonstrated by the many, often quite entertaining anecdotes that Benvenuto narrates in his commentary, which reinforce the image of a relationship founded on an authentic affection.[6] As I have said, Benvenuto followed the *lectura Dantis* that Boccaccio held in Florence between 1373 and 1374, and this too was an important event for him, which he frequently recalls in his commentary. The very next year, moreover, Benvenuto launched his first series of lessons on the *Commedia*; there is no doubt that his attendance in Boccaccio's course played, in this sense, a decisive role.

The relationship with Petrarch was on the other hand much less intense: the two met, as Benvenuto recounts, and wrote one another; but it is understood that Benvenuto never developed an affection for Petrarch and an intellectual esteem comparable to those which he held for Boccaccio. Nor did Petrarch, for his part, seem to consider Benvenuto a particularly important interlocutor. The letter that I have cited at the beginning of the previous chapter, the *Sen.* XV.11, furnishes proof of this: Petrarch writes to Benvenuto using the rather formal *vos*, and above all responds to his question – a fundamental question, given that it regards the truth value of poetical invention – in a somewhat cursory fashion. The *Sen.* XV.11 remains in any case an important document, to which I will return again.

While in Maramauro's commentary the names of Petrarch and Boccaccio are simply affixed to that of Dante, in Benvenuto's commentary, which followed Maramauro's by very few years, it is already possible to discern a full consciousness of the centrality of the three authors in the panorama of the 'new' poetry. Benvenuto has moreover a clear opinion regarding the field in which each of the three authors excels. So far as poetic creation is concerned, Dante is evidently the greatest, in his eyes: Dante is the author of a universal work in which every aspect of the knowable is developed in perfect poetic form and is gathered within a solid moral perspective. Let us read a passage from the proem of Benvenuto's commentary:

> No other poet knew how to praise and admonish better than Dante, I
> mean in a most excellent and effective way. . . . He praised virtue and
> virtuous people, he admonished vice and vicious people. He was a per-
> fect poet and he used poetic images in an extremely appropriate way,
> as is clear to anyone who reads his poem.[7]

These words contain a number of interesting points. In the first place, Dante's excellence is founded on the basis of an evaluative criterion that we have found also in the prologue *Dante poeta sovrano*: Dante was the greatest of all in denouncing the vices and exalting the virtues. Boccaccio, too, in his *Trattatello* (first draft, § 176; second draft, § 116), had expressed an analogous opinion: Dante decided to write the *Commedia* "to punish the evildoers with the direst penalties and to honor the virtuous with the highest rewards".[8] But Benvenuto highlights a fundamental detail. Dante does not limit himself to describing the vices and the virtues, but he does so by making use of poetic images, and he makes use of these "in an extremely appropriate way": "convenientissime", as the original text has it. Now, the meaning of this term is fundamental: in what sense are the poetic images elaborated by Dante "appropriate"? Are they appropriate because they transfigure the truth into allegorical form, as Petrarch would prescribe, or are they appropriate for another reason? The response to this question, as can be intuited, plays a decisive role in determining why Benvenuto considers Dante the greatest poet of all times.

Petrarch, too, is often defined by Benvenuto as a 'poet' – "modernus poeta" or "novissimus poeta". But Benvenuto is closely familiar with only the *Bucolicum carmen* out of Petrarch's verse production, and moreover commented this work, as I have said. Benvenuto has heard mention of the *Africa*, but he does not seem to have ever read it.[9] And above all he seems to be entirely ignorant of – or at least seems but minimally to consider – Petrarch's vernacular production. The single reference to the *Rerum vulgarium fragmenta* contained in his commentary is rather generic; this notwithstanding, it is a reference which can offer us certain interesting points for reflection. Benvenuto writes:

> Petrarch loved Lauretta for twenty-one years, as much in reality as in his poetry [*historice et poetice*]. The first fact emerges from his love verses in vernacular; for the second, proof is furnished by his *Bucolicum carmen* and many of his other writings.[10]

It is noteworthy that in this passage the vernacular lyric poems of the *Canzoniere* are interpreted as an immediate mark, so to speak, of the reality of Petrarch's amorous experience and that the *Bucolicum carmen* is rather understood as a work in which the same experience undergoes a radical 'poetic' re-treatment. I will come back to this point, because it is pivotal.

To those few and meagre references to Petrarch's poetic production, in Benvenuto's commentary are counterpoised at least fifteen explicit references to his prose production: the epistles (*Familiares, Seniles, Sine nomine*), the moral writings (*De vita solitaria, Invectiva contra eum qui maledixit Italie, De remediis utriusque fortune*), and the historiographical and geographical texts (*De gestis Cesaris, Itinerarium ad sepulcrum Domini*).[11] In the eyes of Benvenuto, Petrarch is therefore essentially the author of works in Latin prose: he is more an 'orator' than a poet. Benvenuto's commentary on *Par.* I.34–36 is very explicit in this regard. Let us read at first Dante's verses:

> A tiny spark can result in a great flame:
> perhaps, following after me, with better voices,
> others will pray so that Cyrrha will reply.[12]

Benvenuto comments these verses as follows:

> it is as if Dante says: "perhaps there will soon be a poet more eloquent
> than I, who will be able to move Apollo better than I"; and Dante says
> *forse* (*perhaps*), expressing a doubt. You can observe that Dante partially
> speaks the truth: indeed, in the same period in which Dante was in
> full bloom, the new poet Petrarch was just blossoming. Petrarch
> was actually more prolific and eloquent than Dante. But certainly if
> Petrarch was a greater rhetor than Dante, Dante was a better poet than
> Petrarch. And this is easily demonstrated by this holy poem.[13]

The superiority of Dante is affirmed without hesitation. Petrarch as a
writer is, on the whole, more prolific, but his poetic work cannot so much
as rival that of Dante. Benvenuto immediately closes the question: "this is
easily demonstrated by this holy poem"; there is nothing else to be said.
It is important to observe that in the explicit contrast between Dante and
Petrarch proposed by Benvenuto, the question of the language they use is
never broached. It is indeed not his choice of language – or, more generally,
his style – which confers on Dante excellence in poetry. Dante's excellence
is founded on another criterion.

## Against allegory: Benvenuto and his 'maestro' Boccaccio

What is this criterion? To answer this question in an exhaustive way it is
necessary to examine it from afar, so to speak. I have mentioned the friendship which tied Benvenuto to Boccaccio. But in Benvenuto's eyes, Boccaccio is not only a friend: he is a beloved master – "a venerable teacher",
as Benvenuto often repeats – and above all he is a great writer. Boccaccio is the author of the *Decameron*, a book which Benvenuto defines as
*pulcerrimus* – "very beautiful" – and which he cites with some frequency in
his commentary on the *Commedia*.[14] Benvenuto's love for the *Decameron*
also motivates his use of another very significant formula to define Boccaccio: "an attentive investigator of all charming stories". A very similar
formula is used in Benvenuto's comment to define Dante as well: "a very
inquiring investigator of memorable and modern things".[15] We therefore
understand that the centrality of the narration – the importance conferred on
the 'stories', both ancient and modern – is, in Benvenuto's opinion, what unites
Dante and Boccaccio, and what renders both of them superior to Petrarch.
It does not surprise us that Benvenuto defines the author of the *Decameron*
as "an attentive investigator of all charming stories". It is not as obvious,
on the other hand, that the same expression might be used to describe the
peculiar quality of the author of the *Commedia*.

To fully comprehend Benvenuto's criteria of evaluation of Dante's poetry, we must attentively examine his rapport with Boccaccio, and more precisely with Boccaccio the "venerable teacher", who for Benvenuto is essentially Boccaccio the interpreter of Dante. As we know, Benvenuto attended Boccaccio's lessons on the *Commedia*, but he was unable to consult the *Esposizioni*; nonetheless he knew and very frequently used the other work which Boccaccio dedicated to Dante, the *Trattatello*. For Benvenuto, Boccaccio's *Trattatello* is above all an essential source for reconstructing Dante's biography: much of the information about the poet's life gathered by Boccaccio is in fact repeated in precisely the same form in Benvenuto's commentary.[16] But the *Trattatello* is not only this: it is also the book in which Boccaccio proposes his interpretation of the *Commedia* as an allegorical poem, as we have observed in the first chapter of this book. How does Benvenuto react to this interpretation?

The most important page of the *Trattatello* dedicated to the presentation of the allegorical structure of Dante's poem is contained at the end of the book, in both editions (first draft, §§ 222–227; second draft, §§ 151–156). I have already mentioned this page in the first chapter, but it would be well to invoke it briefly now. Boccaccio interprets a prophetic dream of Dante's mother, Bella degli Abati. At the end of this dream there appears a peacock: according to Boccaccio, this peacock prefigures Dante's masterpiece, the *Commedia*. The peacock has four fundamental characteristics that could be applied to Dante's dream as well. We can limit ourselves to examining three of these, reading what Boccaccio writes in the first edition of the *Trattatello*:

1   Angelic plumage (§§ 224–225): "The feathers with which this body is covered I take to mean the beauty of the unique narrative which appears on the literal surface of the *Comedy*: for example, how Dante descended to Hell and saw the structure of the place and the various conditions of the inhabitants. . . . Truly, then, the flesh of our peacock is covered with an angelic plumage".

2   Ugly feet (§ 226): "In the same manner the ugly feet of the peacock . . . conform perfectly to our author's *Comedy*. For since the whole body seems to be supported by the feet, so too, at first sight, it appears that every written work is supported by the spoken word ['il modo del parlare', which we can perhaps translate better as 'natural language']. The vernacular that props up every part of the *Comedy* is ugly in comparison with the elegant and masterful literary style that every other serious poet employs".

3   Incorruptible flesh (§ 222): "I say that the profound meaning of our *Comedy* is symbolically similar to the flesh of the peacock, because

whether you give a moral or theological meaning [= allegorical] to any part of the book that you like most, its truth remains simple and immutable".

It is not difficult to comprehend the ideological meaning of these passages. The "ugly feet" of the peacock represent the vernacular, which is "ugly in comparison with the elegant and masterful literary style that every other serious poet employs", namely, Latin. Boccaccio reacts to this observation, which is an evident concession to Petrarch, by evidencing the allegorical nature of Dante's writing. Points 1 and 3 indeed bring to the foreground the traditional opposition between the literal sense and the allegorical sense. The plumage – the external and superficial part of the peacock's body – represent the literal sense ("the beauty of the unique narrative"); the flesh of the peacock, hidden by the feathers, represents rather the allegorical sense. The truth of the *Commedia* is therefore entirely hidden by the 'plumage'. The style of Dante's poem, which is "ugly" insofar as it is vernacular, is redeemed insofar as it is allegorical, and indeed thanks to its allegorical nature the superficies of the text become as beautiful as the "angelic plumage" of the peacock. But this implies that the truth of the poem is accessible only to few readers: those who have the capacity to see what is hidden beneath the 'plumage' of the text.

Let us now read Benvenuto's adaptation of Bella degli Abati's dream, based on the dream's description in Boccaccio's *Trattatello*, and in particular his reflection on the symbolic value of the three main details of this vision:

1 Angelic plumage: "The peacock has a very beautiful plumage, which dresses and adorns his flesh . . .: we can say the same for the literal sense of this poem, which adorns the concepts with different rhetorical decorations".

2 Ugly feet: "The peacock has ugly feet . . .: we can say the same for the style of this poem, which sustains the subject matter and which can be considered ugly compared to Latin but in its own genre is the most beautiful of all and, moreover, is better suited to modern intellects".

3 Incorruptible flesh: "We can say the same for the fundamental sense of this book, which is fragrant and delightful in all its parts, in the surface as well as in the sentence, because it contains a simple and incorruptible truth".[17]

As can be seen, everything changes in Benvenuto's version. First of all, as we read in point 2, the style – the language – of the *Commedia* is not objectively "ugly" ("turpis"), as Boccaccio asserts, but *might seem* ("videtur") "ugly" as compared to Latin ("stylus . . . literalis"). And nonetheless, in Benvenuto's judgement, the style of Dante is not in the least ugly, because it is excellent in its genre and, beyond this, because it is the language which is best adapted to the comprehensive capacities of the moderns. The "angelic plumage" no longer corresponds, in Benvenuto's version, to the superficial story – to the fiction of the letter, counterpoised to the truth of the allegory – but rather represents simply the rhetorical decoration that adorns Dante's versification ("variis floribus et diversis coloribus"). In fact, Benvenuto makes no mention of the "unique narrative" spoken of by Boccaccio ("how Dante descended to Hell and saw the structure of the place").

But the most important variation regards the image of the incorruptible flesh of the peacock. Boccaccio identifies in this the allegorical sense of the *Commedia*, the hidden "moral or theological" sense; and, according to Boccaccio, the truth of Dante's poem resides only in this sense, in this 'hidden flesh'. According to Benvenuto, on the other hand, the truth of Dante's poem lies in both its levels, both the literal ("superficialiter") as well as that which is properly 'conceptual' ("sententialiter"). The distinction between letter and allegory is thus lost. Benvenuto holds, in other words, that in the *Commedia* there is no hidden truth: the truth is transmitted in an immediate way to the reader, since it is integrally contained already in the external part of the text. This means that according to Benvenuto da Imola the *Commedia* is not an allegorical text: it is a text which contains some allegories but which does not make of allegorical language its single expressive modality.[18]

The reflection on the open and accessible character of Dante re-emerges in many points in Benvenuto's commentary. According to Benvenuto, moreover, Dante wrote his poem for a very simply reason: "to render men better, both by frightening them, by showing to them the terrible punishments of the Hell, and by encouraging them, by revealing to them the joy of the rewards of Paradise".[19] It is an elementary concept, naturally; but it is evident, at the same time, that it can in no way be reconciled with allegorical language – that is, with a language which is not immediately comprehensible. And it is noteworthy that Benvenuto expresses this concept by taking up Boccaccio once more. It is indeed in the *Trattatello* (first draft, § 176) that we read that Dante undertook the writing of the *Commedia* because he wanted "to punish the evildoers with the direst penalties and to honor the virtuous with the highest rewards". Benvenuto translates this passage to the letter in the introduction to his commentary: Dante "intendit . . . gravissimis poenis mordere viciosos et altissimis praemiis honorare virtuosos".[20]

As I have shown in the first chapter, Boccaccio's reflection on the *Commedia* undergoes several oscillations, as much in the *Trattatello* as in the *Esposizioni*: the project of presenting Dante's poem as a radically allegorical work suffers, every so often, from very evident setbacks. Benvenuto wholly grasps Boccaccio's uncertainties and acts in consequence: he takes up the letter of the passages in which Boccaccio admits the total self-sufficiency of the literal sense of the poem, and modifies, so far as to overturn their meaning, the passages in which Boccaccio insists on the allegorical nature of Dante's writing. The interpretation of the dream of Bella degli Abati is, from this point of view, a very eloquent example.

In Benvenuto's commentary, this distancing from the interpretive line of Boccaccio has various consequences. Among these, the first and the most relevant regards Benvenuto's judgement regarding the audience to which Dante intended to write: Benvenuto holds that Dante wrote to be understood by the greatest number of persons possible, and – what is still more important – Benvenuto judges this choice in wholly positive terms. In a gloss on canto IX of the *Inferno*, Benvenuto writes: "I would be very surprised if those who have pleasure in reading this poem do not become better people in their lives".[21] Anyone who reads Dante's *Commedia*, in other words, derives an immediate ethical profit. This passage appears particularly significant if we set it side by side with what Benvenuto asserts in his commentary on Virgil's *Bucolics* and on Petrarch's *Bucolicum carmen*.[22] The bucolic works of Virgil and of Petrarch are extremely clear examples of allegorical poetry: the superficial tale – the 'letter' – in them has no other function than to conceal the true meaning of the text. Benvenuto holds that Virgil and Petrarch decided to employ allegorical figurations as a precaution, that is to defend themselves against possible attacks from powerful men who might be offended by their verses. Virgil adapts this strategy "to freely criticise the vices of the powerful, while sheltering himself from their reaction";[23] and Petrarch did the same, toward the end of "being able to freely and with impunity criticise and admonish the powerful".[24] To all evidence, Dante had no qualms of this kind: as Benvenuto observes in a passage I have already cited, "no other poet knew how to praise and admonish better than Dante, I mean in a most excellent and effective way".

The road chosen by Virgil and Petrarch, on the other hand, proves itself considerably less "effective". Let us read another passage from Benvenuto's commentary on Virgil's *Bucolics*:

> as Petrarch says, referring to the first eclogue of his *Bucolicum carmen*, it is impossible that the reader should understand bucolic poetry if the poet does not help him, by furnishing him with the key to decipher his verses.[25]

Benvenuto is citing the *Fam.* X.4, a letter which Petrarch wrote, as we know, to recount the story of the birth of poetry but also to give his brother

Gherardo an interpretive key for the first eclogue of the *Bucolicum car-men, Parthenias*. Benvenuto very faithfully reproduces Petrarch's words. In *Fam.* X.4, Petrarch indeed writes that bucolic poetry, by its nature, "is such that it must be explained by the author himself to be understood" (§ 12). The precision with which Benvenuto repeats this concept, however, in no way implies agreement, on his part, with the conception of poetry promoted by Petrarch. From Benvenuto's point of view, Petrarch does not actually describe a quality of poetic writing in the *Fam.* X.4 but rather one of its defects – almost one of its contradictions. The poet who must accompany his verses with an explanation to render them comprehensible is certainly inferior to the poet who offers immediate moral benefit to his readers, as Dante indeed does.[26]

## The 'convenientissimae repraesentationes', the 'exempla' and the legitimacy of the vernacular

In Benvenuto's judgement, the effectiveness of the *Commedia* is grounded in the fact that it proposes a teaching that requires no special key to be understood. Let us examine this question more attentively. Before all, Benvenuto explains that the *Commedia* is a work of poetry that takes as its subject the state of the human soul after death – that is, in other words, the three kingdoms of the Christian afterlife.[27] In the rigid and extremely detailed structure of Dante's poem, every human action is judged according to a criterion of justice: the representation of the state of souls after death can therefore be understood as a representation of good and evil in their nature as absolute concepts. Benvenuto observes moreover that Dante does not limit himself to abstractly describing the punishments that will be imposed on the sinners in the afterlife and the awards that will be conferred on the virtuous, thus proposing to the reader simple simulacra of vices and virtues: Dante narrates and judges the actions of human beings who histori-cally existed.

Where, in this portrait, is poetry to be found? What are the *convenien-tissimae repraesentationes* that render Dante the greatest of the poets, as Benvenuto writes in the proem to his commentary? The element of inven-tion, which qualifies the *Commedia* as a work of poetry, can be identified precisely in this projection of earthly history on an ultramundane space. The kingdoms described by Dante are, of course, separate kingdoms in Christian theology, but they can be conceived also as 'poetic images' of the moral conditions of human souls before their separation from the body. The Hell represented by Dante, for instance, is both the space in which the souls of sinners will be gathered after death and also the image of the state of the sinner who yet dwells in the world: Benvenuto writes that "the stained soul of the sinner, united still to their bodies, is in a 'moral' Hell". The same thing can be said of Purgatory and Paradise. The 'moral' Purgatory of Dante represents the condition of him who, in the earthly life, "distances himself from the vices to search for virtue", while the 'moral' Paradise represents the condition of whomever "has reached spiritual perfection . . . already in this wretched world".[28]

The three kingdoms of the afterlife represented in the *Commedia* must be interpreted, therefore, also as poetic images of three conditions which can be referred to the souls of the living – the condition of sin, the condition of purification from sin and the condition of spiritual perfection. The relation which unites the images of the ultramundane kingdoms to the moral conditions of the living is a relation of analogy: the punishments described in Dante's *Inferno*, for example, reproduce the suffering that necessarily accompany vicious actions already in the course of life. In canto VII of the *Inferno*, Dante recounts that the 'iracondi' (the angry) "kept striking each other, and not only with hands, | but with head and breast and feet, | tearing each other apart with their teeth, piece by piece" (vv. 112–114). Observing this torment, Benvenuto notes: "already in earthly life [*in isto mundo*] they suffer this tremendous punishment, since they assault one another, wounding and mutilating one another".[29]

Indeed, the relationship between the dead and the living on which, in Benvenuto's judgement, Dante's entire invention rides, is not in and of itself particularly original. According to an ancient interpretive line, even the classical poets, and in particular Homer and Virgil, had conferred to their representations of the afterlife the same meaning. In a scholium to the sixth book of the *Aeneid*, Servius (fourth to fifth century CE) wrote: "everything which the poets refer to the underworld in their fictions occurs, in reality, in our lives".[30] Almost all the first commentators of Dante's *Commedia* interpret the afterlife described by Dante in this way. Even Boccaccio observes that, beyond the Hell proper, in which the souls of the sinners are gathered after their separation from their bodies, there exists a Hell 'within' the human soul: "Regarding this Hell, poets are in accordance with the theologians and depict it as being in the hearts of men".[31] Departing from these premises, Benvenuto adds a further element – and one of fundamental importance. Dante does not limit himself to establishing a generic bond between the representation of the ultramundane kingdoms and the various moral conditions of the living, as had done the ancient poets: Dante adapts this relation to the concrete biographical reality of every personage cited in the poem.

The biographies of the characters of the *Commedia* are represented through their final consequences, and in this way they assume an absolute value. Dante's Hell, Purgatory and Paradise, in other words, offer to the reader the poetic representation of a definitive judgement on the historical

actions of human beings. To understand and appreciate this judgement, it is
necessary to understand the facts which stand at their origin. The interpreter
of the *Commedia* has the task of demonstrating to the reader the perfect
correspondence between the 'poetic' judgement and the historical truth,
between the placement of a given person in a given place in the afterlife
and the meaning of the actions that characterised his life. To comment the
*Commedia* thus means, in the first place, evidencing the analogical relationship which holds between Dante's poetic invention and the historical
facts which underpin it. The continuity and the harmony – the very *con-
venientia* – which tie the one to the others is the reason for the prestige
of Dante's poem, and it is this which renders Dante not merely "a very
inquiring investigator of memorable and modern things", like Boccaccio,
but also "a perfect poet". There is then a further element which should be
underlined. To know the historical facts upon which Dante's invention rests
not only allows one to appreciate the *convenientissimae repraesentationes*
which render the *Commedia* an excellent poetic text, but it also allows one
to draw a clear moral teaching therefrom.

Benvenuto is actually in the first place a historian and only afterwards
an interpreter of literary works: it should therefore not surprise us that he
identifies in the historical narration of Dante's poem its most important
crux. In a note to canto III of the *Inferno*, Benvenuto observes that Dante,
to describe the various sins by which human beings can stain themselves,
chooses the most emblematic historic personages, "so that their examples
[*eorum exempla*] might more effectively spur the souls of the readers".[32]
From a rhetorical and conceptual point of view, the *exemplum* is the opposite of the allegory: an *exemplum* illustrates a moral notion through a historically true tale; the allegory, meanwhile, hides the moral teaching through
a fable. According to Benvenuto, Dante's *Commedia* is essentially a great
catalogue of *exempla*, of morally meaningful stories, all of whose meanings
are explicit and immediately available. All the souls encountered by Dante
historically incarnate, and without any ambiguity, a vice or a virtue and thus
offer a clear moral teaching, which is much more effective insofar as it is
transmitted in "delightful" forms:

> [Dante] knew how to comprehend the nature of human beings of every
> role, profession and social condition, with exceptional subtlety, and he
> was able to represent all of this in a way which is at one and the same
> time useful and delightful.[33]

In the context of an interpretation of the *Commedia* aimed at highlighting
the open character of Dante's writing, it is quite natural that Benvenuto does
not consider the vernacular inferior to Latin. More still: in Dante's poem,

the variety of the vernacular is evidently useful for 'mapping' the multiplicity of human experiences and offering it a representation which is "at one and the same time useful and delightful". And it is precisely this scrupulous operation of reality-mapping – both mundane and ultramundane – which breaks the traditional connection between the vernacular and the transmission of mutable and ephemeral contents, such as those relating to the passions. According to Benvenuto da Imola, the *Commedia* demonstrates, in short, that it is the contents which confer a character of stability and universality on the style and on the language, and not the other way around.

Petrarch, naturally, would not have approved of these ideas, and Benvenuto well knew it. There were thence two obvious routes open to Benvenuto: ignore the critiques of Petrarch or else address them in plain sight. He opted instead for a third path, and one which is decidedly unbiased. Benvenuto totally overturns Petrarch's judgement on Dante's linguistic choices by making use of precisely that document in which Petrarch had expressed his thought on the *Commedia* in the most explicit way. Let us read a passage from Benvenuto's comment on canto III of the *Inferno*. Why did Dante write his poem in the vernacular? Benvenuto responds as follows:

> There are many reasons. In the first place, Dante wrote in the vernacular to benefit many people. . . . Had he written in Latin, he would have benefited only the literati, and not even all of them, but only some of them. In this way, he realised a work which had never been attempted before, in which the most cultivated men and the wisest men too might find material for their speculations. In the second place, Dante, seeing that the cult of the liberal arts . . . had been abandoned by the sovereigns and the nobles . . ., decided to write in the vernacular, though he had already begun to compose his poem in Latin with these words: 'Ultima regna canam, fluido contermina mundo, | Spiritibus quae lata patent, quae premia solvunt | Pro meritis cuicumque suis', etc. Many hold on the other hand that Dante wrote in the vernacular because he was conscious of the fact that his mastery of the Latin language was not sufficient to tackle so elevated a theme. I, too, would be swayed by this idea, if the modern poet Petrarch had not convinced me otherwise; for he wrote these words regarding Dante to my venerable teacher Boccaccio: 'I heartily agree, since I have the highest esteem for his ability [i.e. Dante's ability], that he could do anything that he undertook'.[34]

Let us attentively reread the passage from Petrarch cited by Benvenuto. In the *Fam.* XXI.15, § 20, Petrarch writes: "I heartily agree, since I have the highest esteem for his ability, that he could do anything that he undertook; but what he did choose to attempt is clear".[35] The first part of the sentence

is, to all evidence, a purely ironic concession: what Petrarch says immediately afterwards – "but what he did choose to attempt is clear" – clearly
demonstrates this. A few paragraphs after this passage, moreover, Petrarch
writes in a totally explicit way that the results obtained by Dante in writing in the Latin tongue were on the whole modest (§ 24). With a simple
omission in the citation from *Fam*. XXI.15, Benvenuto inverts the sense of
Petrarch's thought on Dante's work.[36] And this is a wholly conscious operation, indeed an almost diabolical one: Benvenuto writes that it was Petrarch
himself who convinced him of the fact that Dante could have excelled in
any endeavour, including, thus, writing Latin poetry! The same citation
'borrowed' from the *Fam*. XXI.15 is also found in the oldest version of
Benvenuto's comment, which dates back, as noted, to 1375: "Petrarch says:
'I have the greatest opinion of this man: he knew how to do everything in
an excellent way'".[37]

There are several other elements we must consider. The first part of
the passage that I have transcribed reports the famous legend of Ilaro. It
is interesting to observe that Benvenuto perfectly grasps the potential risk
contained in that legend: it might indeed bring one to believe that Dante
had ceased to write the *Commedia* in Latin hexameters because he was conscious of his inability to pursue such a course. As we know, a few years after
Benvenuto, Filippo Villani would interpret this legend in precisely this way:
he would recount that Dante himself had admitted to not thinking his own
Latin to be up to the heights of the great classic poets.[38] Benvenuto pretends
to have thought of the same thing, and then resolves the problem in the way
that I have illustrated.

In Ilaro's epistle, as we know, the relation between the *Commedia* and the
literati was guaranteed exclusively by the allegorical character of Dante's
writing, and Boccaccio had attempted to follow the same path. Benvenuto
discards this principle. The *Commedia*, according to Benvenuto, can satisfy
the expectations of the cultivated public without having recourse to allegorical maskings. The multiple philosophical investigations that are explicitly
offered to the reader over the course of the poem are the most obvious proof
of this:

> thus, as no good painter can exist who does not have a general com-
> prehension of all things, in the same way there can exist no good poet
> who does not have mastery over the philosophical sciences, and the
> reading of Dante's poem continually demonstrates this, and in a totally
> manifest way.[39]

In the prologue *Dante poeta sovrano* (thus, in Guido da Pisa), the superiority of the *Commedia* over every other poetic work was held to be the

consequence of its admirable combination of different genres in a single text. Benvenuto too recognises this merit to Dante's writing: "we must observe that in this poem are contained both all philosophical knowledge, and all poetic genres".[40] But the significance that Benvenuto attributes to this observation is somewhat different. The sum of all knowledge and all poetic genres is not only a sign of Dante's poetic greatness – it is not merely a 'technical' and aesthetic merit, so to speak, of the *Commedia* – but it is above all proof of the fact that Dante wrote so as to offer to humanity the greatest boon that could be imagined: sure models of comportment for 'simple' readers and occasions for high philosophical, theological and scientific reflection for the wise.

## Short-term effects

The interpretive work of Benvenuto da Imola on the *Commedia* is chronologically located, as I have said, between 1375 and the first half of the following decade. Francesco da Buti and the Anonimo Fiorentino wrote a few years after him. Both were very familiar with Benvenuto's commentary, and indeed made ample use of it.[41] In the previous chapter, we observed that neither Francesco da Buti nor the Anonimo Fiorentino show any particular interest in the critiques that were levelled against the language of the *Commedia*: it is possible that their silence depends also on the fact that Benvenuto, some years prior, had given a great contribution toward the confutation of these critiques.

This does not mean that the interpretive line taken by Benvenuto established the parameters of what followed in any mechanical fashion, or without any 'resistance'. But this notwithstanding, Benvenuto's influence is perceptible in successive commentators, above all in relation to the questions that we have discussed up to now. For example, the Anonimo Fiorentino is shown to be in agreement with Benvenuto, not only in his rejection of the critiques brought against Dante's vernacular but also in avoiding a systematically allegorical reading of the *Commedia* (and the fact is noteworthy, because in his commentary the Anonimo Fiorentino, in contrast to Benvenuto, employed Boccaccio's *Esposizioni*, in which, as we know, a double interpretation is proposed for every canto, first a literal and then an allegorical one). Francesco da Buti, although the devaluation of the vernacular is alien to him, is still more faithful to the Boccaccian model as regards the search for the 'hidden' meanings of the *Commedia* – he even holds that there are readers of Dante's poem who "feel intellectually satisfied only when the allegoric meaning has been illustrated to them".[42] It is not necessarily the case, however, that this opinion is the fruit of a deliberate distancing from the precedent set by Benvenuto. It is more likely that Francesco da Buti, after having selected Boccaccio's commentary as his fundamental model, decided to remain substantially faithful to its general approach. This does not stop him from making frequent use, however, of Benvenuto's commentary as well. And it is significant that Benvenuto's commentary is used by Francesco da Buti above all to illustrate the 'letter' of the *Commedia*, both as regards the unfurling of the historical allusions present in the poem and as regards the evaluation of the properly rhetorical and grammatical aspects of Dante's verses.[43]

There are several other commentators that we must mention. One of these, the Franciscan friar Giovanni Bertoldi da Serravalle, was a direct 'pupil' of Benvenuto da Imola: Giovanni da Serravalle attended the lessons on the *Commedia* held by Benvenuto in Ferrara in the winter of 1375–1376, and he took from those lessons fundamental material to write his own commentary, which was composed some thirty years later, in 1416–1417. Serravalle very faithfully reproduces the essential ideas of his teacher.[44] And yet Serravalle develops a different opinion with respect to Benvenuto on the value of Petrarch. Indeed, Serravalle holds that Petrarch was the "maximus poeta", "the greatest of the poets", though Dante was "sapientior eo", "wiser than him".[45] Serravalle's judgement might be compared to the opinion on Dante and Petrarch that, according to Pietro Bembo (*Prose della volgar lingua* II.20), Niccolò Lelio Cosmico would express various decades after:

> Cosmico, in one of his sonnets, had conferred on Petrarch the second place in poetry. . . . The judgement of Cosmico is based on the loftiness and the breadth of the subject matter [of the *Commedia*]. . . and on the conviction that Dante, in his poem, had treated of many more doctrinal and scientific questions than had Petrarch.[46]

It is curious that Serravalle, beginning from the same premises, reaches a contrary conclusion to that of Cosmico: Dante is wiser than Petrarch, but Petrarch is "maximus poeta". We do not know on what reasoning or by what aesthetic criterion Serravalle's conclusion was founded. In Bembo's *Prose*, the vastness of the material and above all the variety of the style of the *Commedia* are considered to be – contra Cosmico's judgement[47] – grave defects in Dante's writing: "the *Commedia* can be legitimately compared to a vast and beautiful field of grain, in which however the grain is mixed with oats, darnel and other sterile and damaging weeds".[48] It is difficult to believe that Serravalle too thought in this way. However this might be, it is opportune to underline another element: in Serravalle's commentary, regardless of his judgement that Petrarch is the greatest of the poets, no concession is made to Petrarch's ideas on poetry. Just as Benvenuto before him, Serravalle does not in the least despise the vernacular, and above all he rejects the idea that the fundamental teachings of Dante's *Commedia* are hidden beneath an allegorical veil. Commenting on canto IX of the *Inferno*, Serravalle does not hesitate to adopt Benvenuto's words as his own on the facility with which the letter of Dante's poem encourages moral improvement; indeed, he repeats it with a great deal of emphasis: "Truly, I feel I must say, in my quality as a bishop interpreting and commenting Dante's book, that I would be amazed if anyone, in reading and studying this book, did not improve morally".[49]

Some ten years before Serravalle, on the other hand, Filippo Villani had altogether accepted the critiques levelled by the first humanists, and above all by Petrarch, against Dante's vernacular. We have seen what meaning Villani confers on the legend of friar Ilaro – the contrary meaning with respect to that given by Boccaccio (and Benvenuto da Imola). Moreover, Filippo Villani had made himself the promoter of a strongly allegorical interpretation of the *Commedia*.[50] This notwithstanding, even Villani had to admit that the fundamental crux of the meaning of Dante's poem appears immediately evident to the reader, since it is entrusted to an element which, by its very nature, is the very contrary of allegorical fictions. Villani indeed recognises that at the heart of the *Commedia* one finds the historical actions of those personages cited by Dante, and that the most important teachings transmitted by the poet to his readers are entrusted precisely to the clear moral judgement expressed in those actions.[51]

The appreciation for the centrality of the human story in Dante's invention and of its spontaneous pedagogical value is without doubt the most important heritage that Benvenuto left to the readers of Dante in successive decades. And it might be said that it was precisely this appreciation which constituted the most effective reaction to the critiques that Petrarch and his humanist followers had turned against the *Commedia*. Benvenuto seems to perfectly grasp the risks inherent to Petrarch's ideas on poetry. The first is the most immediate and evident: the contempt for the vernacular could injure, in the long run, the fortune and the diffusion of the *Commedia* – and of other masterpieces of the vernacular literature, such as the *Decameron* – among the cultivated readers. Nor must we underestimate the second risk, which is the reverse side of the first. In the eyes of Benvenuto, the elitism of Petrarch and the first humanists – the idea, that is, that the poets should write for a select readership – cannot help but constitute an obstacle to the wide 'social' benefit offered by Dante's poem. The value of a poetic work indeed resides, according to Benvenuto, in the 'sense' and not in the 'form'; style has no autonomous value; it has value only as a means to render the transmission of a teaching more 'delightful'. Even Petrarch (as well as Boccaccio) shares the same principle. The position of Pietro Bembo on the other hand was to be entirely different, as well as that of those who, over the course of the sixteenth century, would reflect on the canon of the *Tre Corone* especially from an aesthetic point of view. But while Petrarch never negates the moral function of poetry, he certainly excludes that it might benefit the world "that lives ill" (*Purg.* XXXII.103), as Dante held: indeed, according to Petrarch the activity of the poet implicates, by its very nature, a radical detachment from the world.[52]

In this way, we approach another important question, to which I will dedicate the final chapter of this book. The clean-cut opposition on the part of Benvenuto da Imola to Petrarch as theoretician of poetry did not bring an end to the influence which Petrarch exercised on the reception of Dante at the end of the fourteenth century (but also on the reception of Boccaccio's works in vernacular, as we will be able to verify). Side by side with Petrarch the theoretician of poetry, there stands Petrarch the writer of moral works and historical works. And we perceive that, the 'first' having been rejected by virtue of the centrality Dante gave to historical facts and their moral interpretation, for the 'second' a new way opens spontaneously for exercising influence on the interpretation of the *Commedia*. Petrarch indeed has a well-defined opinion not only as regards the language of Dante's poem but also as regards the historical events collected in the *Commedia*, the judgements pronounced on these same events and on their significance. As we will see in the next pages, Benvenuto will have a much harder time opposing Petrarch the historian and moralist than he did Petrarch the theoretician of poetry: and this will have no minor consequences concerning the interpretation of Dante's poem.

## Notes

1 Let us recall, for example, the assimilation of the *Commedia* to the *Bucolicum carmen* as both pertaining to the domain of allegorical language, as asserted both in the *Geneal. Deor. Gent.* XIV.8, § 22, and in the *Esposizioni sopra la "Comedia"*, ad *Inf.* I.73.

2 On the biography of Benvenuto da Imola, see P. Pasquino, 'Benvenuto Rambaldi da Imola', in *Censimento dei commenti danteschi*, ed. by E. Malato and A. Mazzucchi, vol. 1, *I commenti di tradizione manoscritta (fino al 1428)* (Rome: Salerno, 2011), tome 1, 86–88.

3 A rich inventory of manuscripts of Benvenuto da Imola's works has recently been published by M. Daleffe and L. C. Rossi, *Inventario dei manoscritti delle opere di Benvenuto da Imola* (Bergamo: Bergamo University Press-Sestante, 2018).

4 See Benvenuto da Imola, *Lectura Dantis Bononiensis*, ed. by P. Pasquino (Ravenna: Longo, 2017).

5 See Benvenuto da Imola, *Comentum super Dantis Aldigherij "Comoediam"*, ed. by G. F. Lacaita, 5 tomes (Florence: Barbera, 1887).

6 See for example those examined by L. C. Rossi, *Studi su Benvenuto da Imola* (Florence: SISMEL Edizioni del Galluzzo, 2016), 214–215.

7  Benvenuto da Imola, *Comentum*, tome 1, 9.
8  As in the first chapter of this book, I here employ the translation of Vincenzo Zin Bollettino: see G. Boccaccio, *The Life of Dante*, trans. by V. Zin Bollettino (New York-London: Garland, 1990).
9  See Rossi, *Studi su Benvenuto da Imola*, 154–155.
10  Benvenuto da Imola, *Comentum*, tome 1, 83 (*ad Inf.* II.52–54). See L. C. Rossi, 'Presenze di Petrarca in commenti danteschi fra Tre e Quattrocento', *Aevum* 70/3 (1996), 450.
11  See Rossi, 'Presenze di Petrarca', 449–459, *Studi su Benvenuto da Imola*, 181–183, and L. Fiorentini, *Per Benvenuto da Imola* (Bologna: il Mulino, 2016), 91–99, 183, 320–325.
12  I follow once more the translation of Robert M. Durling: see in this case *The Divine Comedy of Dante Alighieri*, III, *Paradiso*, ed. and trans. by R. M. Durling, introduction and notes by R. L. Martinez and R. M. Durling (New York-Oxford: Oxford University Press, 2011).
13  Benvenuto da Imola, *Comentum*, tome 4, 309.
14  See Benvenuto da Imola, *Comentum*, tome 3, 169 (*ad Purg.* VI.13–15). In the next chapter, I will cite some of the novellas of the *Decameron* which Benvenuto uses to interpret the *Commedia*.
15  Benvenuto da Imola, *Comentum*, tome 3, 392 (*ad Purg.* XIV.106–108), tome 3, 526 (*ad Purg.* XX 52–60) and tome 4, 292 (*ad Par.* I, intr.).
16  See Rossi, *Studi su Benvenuto da Imola*, 212–213, Fiorentini, *Per Benvenuto da Imola*, 501–538, and 'Archaeology of the *Tre Corone*', *Dante Studies* 136 (2018), 8.
17  Benvenuto da Imola, *Comentum*, tome 1, 14.
18  On Benvenuto's version of Bella degli Abati's dream, see also Z. G. Barański, 'Boccaccio, Benvenuto e il sogno della madre di Dante incinta', in *"Chiosar con altro testo". Leggere Dante nel Trecento* (Fiesole: Cadmo, 2001), 99–116, and D. Pantone, 'Il pastore e i "piè sozzi" del pavone. Benvenuto *vs* Boccaccio', *Bollettino dantesco* 2 (2013), 17–26.
19  Benvenuto da Imola, *Comentum*, tome 1, 17.
20  Benvenuto da Imola, *Comentum*, tome 1, 17.
21  Benvenuto da Imola, *Comentum*, tome 1, 315 (*ad Inf.* IX.54).
22  Among the most recent studies on the commentaries of Benvenuto on Virgil and Petrarch, see M. L. Lord, 'The Commentary on Virgil's *Eclogues* by Benvenuto da Imola: A Comparative Study of the *Recollectiones*', *Euphrosyne* 22 (1994), 373–401, and 'Benvenuto da Imola's literary approach to Virgil's *Eclogues*', *Medieval Studies* 64 (2002), 287–362, and then G. Cascio, 'Benvenuto da Imola e il *Bucolicum carmen* del Petrarca', in *Petrarca, l'Italia, l'Europa*, ed. by E. Tinelli (Bari: Edizioni di Pagina, 2015), 124–130. See also Rossi, *Studi su Benvenuto da Imola*, 151–161, and Fiorentini, *Per Benvenuto da Imola*, 189–200.
23  See manuscript 109 of the Biblioteca Statale di Cremona, f. 1r: "ut licenter et impune detegat uicia potentum et magnatum".
24  See manuscript Fonds Latin 8700 of the Bibliothèque Nationale de France, f. 1rb: "ut auctor iste alios possit licenter arguere et impune magnates et potentes".
25  See manuscript 109 of the Biblioteca Statale di Cremona, f. 13v (*ad Buc.* III.1): "sicut dicit Petrarca super eglogam suam primam, est impossibile quod aliquis intelligat bucolica nisi habeat aliquid ab illo qui composuit".
26  See Fiorentini, *Per Benvenuto da Imola*, 199–200.

82    *Against Petrarch, theoretician of poetry*

27  The idea that the fundamental subject of the *Commedia* is 'the state of souls after death', and not Dante's ultramundane voyage, dates back to the *Epistle to Cangrande della Scala*, a text which exercised a great influence over the initial reception of Dante's poem: see Fiorentini, *Per Benvenuto da Imola*, 117–150.

28  Benvenuto repeats the same concept in all three versions of his comment. The formulae that I have cited derive from the second edition, which is to say from the *recollectae* of the course on the *Commedia* held by Benvenuto in Ferrara in 1376–1376: see manuscript Ashburnham 839 of the Biblioteca Medicea Laurenziana of Florence, ff. 2*v*-3*r*. See also Benvenuto da Imola, *Lectura Dantis Bononiensis*, 106, and Benvenuto da Imola, *Comentum*, tome 1, 15–16. For a more exhaustive treatment of this subject, see Fiorentini, *Per Benvenuto da Imola*, 1–176.

29  Benvenuto da Imola, *Comentum*, tome 1, 269 (*ad Inf.* VII.112–114). See L. Fiorentini and D. Parisi, 'Chiaroscuri dalla prima ricezione di Dante presso gli ordini mendicanti', *La cultura* 57/2 (2019), 194–198.

30  Servii, *In Vergilii "Aeneidos" librorum commentarii*, ed. by G. Thilo and H. Hagen, 4 vols. (Leipzig: Teubner, 1878–84), vol. 3, 82 (*ad Aen.* VI.596). The translation is mine. On this, see A. Setaioli, *La vicenda dell'anima nel commento di Servio a Virgilio* (Frankfurt am Main: P. Lang, 1995), 173–205.

31  *Esposizioni sopra la "Comedia"*, *accessus*, § 47. I cite here as well the translation of Michael Papio, *Boccaccio's "Expositions" on Dante's "Comedy"*, trans. by M. Papio (Toronto-Buffalo-London: University of Toronto Press, 2009).

32  Benvenuto da Imola, *Comentum*, tome 1, 117.

33  Benvenuto da Imola, *Comentum*, tome 2, 414 (*ad Inf.* XXIX 138–139).

34  Benvenuto da Imola, *Comentum*, tome 1, 78–79 (*ad Inf.* II.10–12).

35  I cite here once again the translation of Aldo S. Bernardo: F. Petrarca, *Letters on Familiar Matters, Rerum familiarum libri XVI–XXIV*, trans. by A. S. Bernardo (Baltimore-London: The Johns Hopkins University Press, 1985), 202–207.

36  See R. Mercuri, 'Percorsi letterari e tipologie culturali nell'esegesi dantesca di Benvenuto da Imola', in *Benvenuto da Imola lettore degli antichi e dei moderni*, ed. by P. Palmieri and C. Paolazzi (Ravenna: Longo, 1991), 61.

37  Benvenuto da Imola, *Lectura Dantis Bononiensis*, 108.

38  See F. Villani, *Expositio seu Comentum super "Comedia" Dantis Allegherii*, ed. by S. Bellomo (Florence: Le Lettere, 1989), 76–77. I have transcribed, translated and commented on this passage in the first chapter of this book.

39  Benvenuto da Imola, *Comentum*, tome 1, 159 (*ad Inf.* IV.110).

40  Benvenuto da Imola, *Comentum*, tome 1, 19 (*Preface*).

41  On the numerous references to Benvenuto in Francesco da Buti's commentary, see Franceschini, 'Francesco da Buti', in *Censimento dei commenti danteschi*, tome 1, 201–202. So far as Benvenuto's presence in the commentary of the Anonimo Fiorentino goes, see Geymonat, 'Anonimo Fiorentino', in *Censimento dei commenti danteschi*, tome 1, 36.

42  Francesco da Buti, *Commento sopra la "Divina Commedia" di Dante Allighieri*, ed. by C. Giannini, 3 tomes (Pisa: Fratelli Nistri, 1858–1862), tome 1, 5.

43  See Franceschini, 'Francesco da Buti', 201–202.

44  See Fiorentini–Parisi, 'Chiaroscuri', 198–200 (with the bibliography).

45  See C. Dionisotti, 'Dante nel Quattrocento (1965)', in *Scritti di storia della Letteratura Italiana*, ed. by T. Basile, V. Fera and S. Villari, vol. 2 (Rome: Edizioni di Storia e Letteratura, 2009), 181.

46  P. Bembo, *Prose della volgar lingua. L'editio princeps del 1525 riscontrata con l'autografo Vaticano Latino 3210*, ed. by C. Vela (Bologna: CLUEB, 2001), 103. Translation is mine.

47 See M. Corrado, 'Niccolò Lelio Cosmico', in *Censimento dei commenti danteschi*, tome 1, 368–369.
48 Bembo, *Prose*, 104.
49 I quote (and directly translate) from the edition of Serravalle's commentary by M. Da Civezza and T. Domenichelli – Giovanni da Serravalle, *Translatio et comentum totius libri Dantis Aldighierii* (Prato: Giachetti, 1891) – taking the citation from the *corpus* of the *Dartmouth Dante Project*.
50 See S. Bellomo, '"La natura delle cose aromatiche" e il sapore della *Commedia*', *Critica del testo* 14/1 (2011), 538.
51 See the discussion on this point in Fiorentini, *Per Benvenuto da Imola*, 163–166.
52 See S. Gentili, 'Petrarca e la filosofia', in *La filosofia in Italia al tempo di Dante*, ed. by C. Casagrande and G. Fioravanti (Bologna: il Mulino, 2016), 264–280.

# 4 Contempt for the present
## The revenge of Petrarch
## the moralist and historian

### Against the modern characters of the *Commedia*

Celestine V was not pusillanimous (*Inf.* III.58–60), but magnanimous (*De vita solitaria* II-8).[1] Averroes was not a noble philosopher (*Inf.* IV.144), but an infamous enemy of Christ (*De otio religioso* I.4, §§ 117–118, and second *Invectiva contra medicum*, § 239).[2] I have already examined, in my previous works, some cases in which the influence of Petrarch forces Benvenuto to distance himself from Dante's judgement regarding certain historical characters; and in the case of Celestine this has important consequences also on a broader interpretive level.[3] But the problems relative to the historical examples contained in the *Commedia* are not limited to Celestine and Averroes. Benvenuto also makes explicit reference to another arduous problem – of a general nature. In a gloss on canto XXVII of the *Inferno*, Benvenuto takes up a critique levelled against Dante's choice to give space, in his poem, to modern events and characters: "every day I find men saying: 'Why did Dante mention this modern man or this modern episode? He would have done better to write about the illustrious men of ancient times!'".[4]

The reference is to the episode of Guido da Montefeltro (died in 1298 circa), which is narrated in canto XXVII of the *Inferno*, offering Benvenuto the occasion to quote these words. Naturally, Benvenuto does not limit himself to quoting them: he carefully examines them, and attempts to refute them. Let us concentrate on these pages of Benvenuto's commentary, following his reasoning step by step. With a conscious excess of subtlety, Benvenuto had previously observed that the first words pronounced by Guido da Montefeltro might allude to a problem of 'poetic' nature. Speaking to Virgil, Guido says (*Inf.* XXVII.22–23):

'though I have arrived perhaps somewhat late,
let it not grieve you to stay and speak with me;
you see it does not grieve me, and I am burning!';[5]

and Benvenuto in turn observes:

> Here we might simply understand that this man did not present himself
> to the two travellers, Dante and Virgil, immediately after their encoun-
> ter with Ulysses [i.e. *Inf.* XXVI.76–142], but delayed a bit. But the
> words of Guido da Montefeltro can be interpreted also in a subtler way.
> I believe indeed that this man wished to say, quietly, 'Though I do not
> belong to that happy time in which you, Virgil, and the other great poets
> gave eternal fame to illustrious men, I deserve nonetheless some sort of
> fame, or at least I deserve my deeds to be recounted'.[6]

The interpretation of Guido da Montefeltro's words proposed by Benvenuto is certainly incorrect; it offers however an occasion for the commentator to express a question of great importance. This question can be briefly
stated in these terms: is it the intrinsic value of a historical character that
renders him illustrious, or is it rather the quality of the voice of the poets who
have sung him? At a first reading, it would appear that the answer is clear:
the value of the ancients depends for the most part on the literary elaboration which had been made of them over the course of time, and above all
it depends on the fortune which they have enjoyed among those authors
contemporary with them. According to Benvenuto, Guido indeed admits,
whilst speaking to Virgil: "I do not belong to that happy time in which you,
Virgil, and the other great poets have given eternal fame to illustrious men".
That is to say, as we might paraphrase, 'Compared to Ulysses, I am a virgin
character from the literary point of view'.
Benvenuto's subsequent reasoning however brings to the surface a mild
uncertainty, or at least it provides space to a complication. If Ulysses' celeb-
rity is given by the verses of poets more than the concrete value of his
deeds, it is on the other hand by virtue of an objective historical quality
that Guido is a candidate for inclusion in a work of poetry. In the second
draft of his commentary, Benvenuto has Guido da Montefeltro say: "I have
accomplished deeds so great that anyone could write of me"; and then Benvenuto adds: "I believe in fact that Guido was a man of greater value than
Ulysses".[7] In short: the value of the ancients is indistinguishable from the
literary re-elaboration of their actions; that value is nothing other, in reality,
than the result of such elaboration. It would seem on the other hand that the
moderns, if they are to prove worthy of being sung by the poets, must excel
at the level of history, demonstrating themselves to be 'illustrious' already
in their own time. But even this conclusion is only partially true, as can
be seen by reading another passage from the same page of Benvenuto's
commentary. Taking his bearings from an anecdote contained in Cicero's

oration *For the poet Archias* (§ 24) – a source to which I will return – Benvenuto writes:

> I have no doubt about the fact the Ulysses is more famous [than Guido da Montefeltro], since great poets have written about him: Homer wrote of him in Greek, Virgil in Latin. In the oration that Cicero composed for the poet Archias, he tells us that Alexander the Great, standing before the tomb of Achilles, exclaimed: 'O lucky youth, who was celebrated by so great a singer!', by whom he meant the poet Homer. And it is as if Alexander wished to say: 'I would there were another Homer to tell of my deeds, granting me eternal fame, as happened to Achilles'. Guido da Montefeltro expresses the same concept. But Guido certainly found an excellent poet, even better than what he deserved: namely, Dante.[8]

The desire for fame belongs to the human beings of all times: already Alexander the Great envied Achilles for being celebrated by Homer. But the example quoted by Benvenuto has other implications as well. First of all, the lament of Alexander at Achilles' tomb relativises the contrast between ancient and modern men so far as to eliminate it: even an illustrious ancient like Alexander the Great – as is obvious – could not but be considered modern when compared to certain other figures. But what is most important is that such perception was founded, already at the time of the Macedonian, on the worship of an idealised past, and more precisely on the conviction that the capacity to magnify the great human endeavours, as found in the works of the ancient poets, was no more. Benvenuto omitted the Ciceronian source, which in this context offered an important indication. Cicero wrote that Alexander conducted his military campaigns in the company of "numbers of epic poets and historians"[9] and that none of them appeared to be of a sufficient level to confer on him the glory that Achilles had obtained through Homer: "Alexander the Great carried in his train numbers of epic poets and historians. And yet, standing before the tomb of Achilles at Sigeum, he exclaimed: 'Fortunate youth, to have found in Homer an herald of thy valour!'". The same indignation tormented Guido da Montefeltro, who, we understand, is twice deceived. He does not understand that the man Virgil is accompanying, namely Dante, is a living man (*Inf.* XXVII.61–66), and above all he is ignorant of the fact that this man is one of the greatest poets that humanity has ever known.

No other commentator, before Benvenuto, has caught in Guido da Montefeltro's words the same meaning that Benvenuto did – which is to say, a reflection on the relation between 'illustrious men' and the fame conferred on them by the poets. Above all, none of the first Dante interpreters makes the least mention of the criticism, recorded by Benvenuto, against

Dante's choice to mention modern men and events in his poem. What is the source of this criticism? We do not know. But naturally I will try to formulate some hypotheses. Certainly, the aversion toward modernity does not belong to any of the commentators of the *Commedia* that are known to us: indeed, among these latter there is a widespread conviction that one of the great merits of the *Commedia* lies in the fact that both ancient and modern characters are cited in it. I recall, for example, the prologue *Dante poeta sovrano*: "[Dante] was also an excellent tragic poet, because he tells about great memorable facts, that have as their protagonists princes and kings, both from ancient and modern times".

The identity of the "homines" ("men") cited by Benvenuto therefore remains unknown. On closer inspection, it is not certain that Benvenuto refers to real interlocutors: the men to whom he refers might be fictitious. However, even if that is the case, the problem remains unsolved. What is the origin of the critique indicated by Benvenuto? As I have said, it does not originate with any known interpreters of the poem. But if it is not possible to give a name to these individuals, can we at least try to circumscribe the cultural circles to which they – real or fictitious as they were – pertained? Or even only to clarify the sense and the origin of their reproach?

## The humanists and modern history

The objections levelled against the representation of modern events and personages could be approached to humanistic environments. But the two intellectuals most closely tied to the nascent humanism with whom Benvenuto entertained relations prove to be totally foreign to the opposition of values between the ancients and the moderns. Giovanni del Virgilio, whom Benvenuto knew for his commentaries on Virgil's *Georgics* and Ovid's *Metamorphoses*,[10] would invite Dante himself to compose a poem in Latin on the protagonists of very recent events (*Ecl.* I.25–34). It is equally farfetched to think that at the origin of the polemic was Coluccio Salutati, to whom Benvenuto grew nearer above all in the last years of his life.[11] In the letter to Niccolò da Teoderano of 2 October 1399 (*Ep.* XI.10), Salutati, listing the qualities of the *Commedia*, lingered on the value that Dante confers to the human actions of every epoch:

> in the *Commedia*, laws, customs, languages and the human actions of all times and of all peoples shine bright as a starry sky, with extraordinary majesty. No other poet can ever surpass nor equal Dante in his style.[12]

In the second book of the *Dialogi ad Petrum Paulum Histrum* of Leonardo Bruni, Niccolò Niccoli, who at an earlier time had expressed himself in extremely negative terms on Dante (First Book, § 44),[13] changes his mind and praises Dante's masterpiece, the *Commedia*, in no uncertain terms. Niccoli initially makes use of a formula which is very similar to that of Salutati which I have just cited (§ 70); he then continues by praising the knowledge that Dante had of both ancient and modern history (§ 72). All the personages of the *Commedia*, Niccoli affirms, were the protagonists of memorable events, and as such are mentioned by the poet. Actions worthy of recollection therefore know no chronological limits; it is indeed one of the signs of Dante's greatness that he was able to recognise and then to order (which is to say, judge) "in a wholly befitting way" ("percommode") events belonging to various times and places (the distinction between "Italian" and "foreign" events – "domestica" and "externa", in the original – is a clear reference to the structure of Valerius Maximus's *Memorable deeds and sayings*).[14] For his part, Leonardo Bruni would write, with evident admiration, that Dante, in his *Commedia*, demonstrates not only an excellent knowledge of "ancient histories" but also "such a vast competency with modern history that it seems as if he had seen, as a direct witness, everything he recounts in his poem".[15]

None of the humanists whom Benvenuto knew personally or of whom he had read the works ever expresses a critique like that recorded in the comment to *Inf.* XXVII. But, as we have seen, even widening our analysis to the humanists who came after Benvenuto, the critiques against the modern personages of the *Commedia* find no concrete match: the "homines" cited by Benvenuto seem to have the consistency of ghosts. And yet Benvenuto is not the only one to defend Dante from those who accused him of having dedicated too much space to modern history in his poem. There is a very interesting text, from this point of view, composed around 1398–1400, less than twenty years after Benvenuto's commentary. This text is entitled *Invective against those who have discredited Dante, Petrarch and Boccaccio*; it was originally drafted in Latin, but today we possess only the vernacular translation. The author was a poet from Florence born around 1350: his name is Cino Rinuccini.[16]

In his *Invective*, Rinuccini accuses some of his contemporaries of having contempt for the great authors of the previous generation, by whom he means our *Tre Corone*: Dante, Petrarch and Boccaccio. Rinuccini, like Giovanni Gherardi, is essentially a 'traditionalist'. He opposes the attitude of rupture with the past adopted by humanism and reaffirms the centrality of scholastic culture: the *Invective* can therefore be read as a document "of the philosophico-literary polemic between defenders and accusers of the old medieval culture and of the vernacular tradition".[17] Rinuccini reprimands his adversaries for various things. Above all, they have unjust contempt for the vernacular of Dante and Boccaccio: they hold that the first is a "poet for cobblers" and that the second "did not know Latin".[18] So far, it is easy to ascribe a precise identity to Rinuccini's adversaries. We know that Leonardo Bruni, for example, judged Dante incapable of writing in a Latin worthy of the great models of antiquity.[19] Filippo Villani too thought the same thing, as we have seen. And Niccolò Niccoli, before radically changing his opinion, had defined Dante as a poet worthy "of the wool workers, the millers and the commoners in general" (*Dialogi ad Petrum Paulum Histrum* I, § 44).[20]

In Rinuccini's *Invective*, however, another argument is evoked which is used by the detractors of the *Tre Corone*. This argument is less obvious, given that it finds no parallel in the works of the humanists that we know; on the other hand, it can be set side by side, as I have already suggested, with the commentary of Benvenuto da Imola on *Inf.* XXVII.16–23. Rinuccini rails against those who consider Dante a "poet for cobblers", and in order to respond to this disparaging judgement he lists the *Commedia*'s qualities. Among these, "all the stories" that Dante narrates to his readers to teach them how to "live in a virtuous way" stand out particularly. In this regard, Rinuccini adds:

> So far as the comparison between Dante and Virgil goes, let Dante's detractors respond sincerely to the following question: has not Dante collected in his poem far more ancient stories than Virgil? They cannot deny it; indeed, it is clear that in Dante's *Inferno* alone, there are more ancient stories than in Virgil's entire work. Regarding modern stories, there is not one worthy of memory which Dante has not cited.[21]

From Rinuccini's words, we can intuit that someone or other had accused Dante of not having given enough space to ancient history in the *Commedia*; and we understand that the accusation presupposes that Dante did not give enough space to ancient history because he did not know enough about it. Rinuccini replies as we have seen. But what he adds immediately afterwards regarding modern history, and the way in which it is treated in the *Commedia*, is also of note. Rinuccini asserts that all the modern events which deserve to be remembered are cited in the *Commedia*. What accusation is Rinuccini responding to with this observation? Certainly, an accusation that must be very similar to that reported by Benvenuto. But perhaps the words of Rinuccini allow us to formulate some further conjecture on this score. Just as Niccolò Niccoli in his retraction, Rinuccini insists on the fact that Dante cited only modern events "degni di fama", "worthy of memory", in his poem: there is no reason to exclude the possibility that the targets of Rinuccini's *Invective* considered the modern events and personages cited by Dante to be unworthy of recollection precisely *because* they are modern.

## Toward the origins of a radical critique

As can be intuited, this conviction is not without its consequences on the plane of literary criticism: to assert that the ancients have a greater literary dignity than the moderns means to draw a very clear confining line around the historical facts meriting inclusion within a work of poetry. It seems in short that the cult for the protagonists of ancient history presupposes the conviction that the moderns have nothing to show for themselves – that is, that their deeds are nothing more than the expression of pure contingency. Taking the words relayed by Benvenuto at face value, Dante's critics do not understand what the function – and therefore, so to speak, the value – of the modern personages in the *Commedia* might be: "*Why* did Dante mention this modern man or this modern episode?" This is the point on which we must pause. To the concept of 'modernity', as we have already seen, Benvenuto in his commentary counterpoises the concept of 'illustrious': "He would have done better to write about the illustrious men of ancient times!" According to Benvenuto, as we will see, such a counterposition is the result of an optical illusion. It is important at this point to establish how this illusion might come about, why it persists and what it really implies.

Toward this end, it might be useful to turn our attention to the reflections elaborated by Boccaccio and Petrarch regarding the narration of memorable historical facts. Let us begin with Boccaccio. In the *Proemio* of the *Decameron*, Boccaccio asserts that the hundred novellas gathered in his book will treat of events that occurred "in times as well modern as ancient" (§ 14),[22] and this means, evidently, that in Boccaccio's eyes antiquity and modernity have the same dignity: what matters is the content of the novella, not the epoch in which its events unfolded. Whoever has read the *Decameron* well knows, moreover, that the novellas set in the modern epoch are much more numerous than those set in ancient times. I will return to the *Decameron* again, because it is, naturally, a crucial text, and its reception by the first of Dante's commentators will give us very interesting information on the position held by Boccaccio as an author – and not only as a mediator between Petrarch and Dante – in the earliest phase of the history of the canon of the *Tre Corone*.

Petrarch's position is decidedly more complex. In September of 1342, responding to Giovanni Colonna, who accused him of having recourse with excessive frequency to the examples of ancient men, Petrarch wrote (*Fam.* VI.4, §§ 1–2):

> I do use great numbers of examples but they are all illustrious, true, and, unless I am mistaken, contain both pleasure and authority. . . . I speak a great deal, I even write a great deal not in order to be of any

particular use to my times, whose wretchedness has reached the point of despair, as to unburden myself of ideas and to console my mind with writing.[23]

Together with experience, the example of the ancients offers a "useful instrument for measuring one's own capacity to resist the blows of fortune and the assault of contemporary mediocrity".[24] In these passages, Petrarch gives expression to a recurring theme in his work: the theme of the painful exile of the moderns from the 'fatherland' of antiquity, which cannot be separated from the feeling of an irremediable distance between the present time and the greatness of an idealised past.[25] The letter to Giovanni Colonna continues: the examples "of famous men of antiquity", just as they benefit Petrarch, can be of benefit also to others (§ 7); so far as the conservation of the memory of ancient history goes, there is no doubt that the written word exceeds any other method in efficacy (§ 11).

It has been said that one of the tasks to which Petrarch dedicated himself "for all of his life",[26] was to restoring a continuity of values, by rendering once more current the patrimony of ancient history. But in the *Fam.* VI.4, as in other places (for example in the letter *To Posterity*, § 9), this motif assumes bitterly polemical tones. And Petrarch is not unconscious of the radical alternative that he sets before his interlocutor: the "exempla clarorum hominum" (§ 3) serve in the first place to forget the present ("I . . . willingly forget those among whom my unlucky star destined me to live; and to flee from these I concentrate all my strength following ancients instead", § 5). Petrarch explains that historical narrative must portray the endeavours, the customs and the traits of the interior life of the ancients; the writer of history therefore must not have any other concern than that of offering his readers images of the ancient virtues (§ 11). As one can intuit, these words imply a neat division. To describe anything other than the "examples of famous men of antiquity" would indeed produce an impoverishment – or even a misunderstanding – of the function of exemplary literature. And it is not a secondary point that the limpid fixity of illustrious examples is counterpoised, in Petrarch's words, to the misery of the present. Petrarch hopes that the contemporary misery is destined to fall into oblivion, but we understand that it would not lend itself to narration, given that, in Petrarch's eyes, it is manifestly inadequate for generating events worthy of remembrance.

In the passages of the *Fam.* VI.4 that we have read, we can easily recognise certain traits which recur from Petrarch's reflections on poetry and, more precisely, his rejection of those forms of literary creation that do not shun the instability of the world. As Petrarch reiterates more than once, when Boethius, in his *Consolation of Philosophy* (I pr. 1, § 8), defines the Muses of poetry as *scenicae meretriculae*, he alludes precisely to this genre of

literature. The despicable 'theatrical' poets offer a representation of everything which is subject to becoming, the passions above all. They neglect to
describe "the nature of people and the world, the virtues, and human perfection", which is to say, the only subjects which offer a sure shelter from the
fickleness of earthly things (third *Invectiva contra medicum*, §§ 116–121).[27]

The same concept is repeated by Petrarch also in the *Sen.* XV.11, which
was addressed to Benvenuto da Imola. It had been Benvenuto, we intuit,
to first evoke in his own letter to Petrarch – which today is lost – the initial pages of Boethius' *Consolation*, most likely asking Petrarch to reas-
sure him of the fact that poetry, as opposed to what Boethius appears to
hold, can be the vehicle of absolute truths. Petrarch responded to him in
this way: "For the rest, I do not change my opinion: whatever is rightly said
[by Boethius] against poets applies to dramatists".[28] In the final draft of the
epistle, Petrarch adds (§ 18): "Quite often – I admit – the language of poets
is bad; why would it not be, since their life too is the worst?"[29] In Petrarch's
judgement, bad poetry, in the last analysis, is precisely this: an uncontrolled
imitation of life.

Benvenuto would share this principle to such an extent that he applied
it even to Petrarch himself. In his commentary on the *Commedia*, Benvenuto would indeed write that Dante was the first poet to use the vernacular
to treat of an "elevated and honest" subject matter.[30] Benvenuto explains
that, before Dante, the vernacular poets wrote only to give vent to their
passions: nothing distinguished those poets, in short, from the "dramatists"
so despised by Boethius and Petrarch. Then Dante arrived, and everything
changed. This notwithstanding, Petrarch continued to write in the vernacular according to the 'old manner', creating thereby a short-circuit between
passion and poetic expression. As Benvenuto observes in another passage
that I have already quoted, "Petrarch loved Lauretta for twenty-one years, as
much in reality as in his poetry. The first fact emerges from his love verses
in vernacular; for the second, proof is furnished by his *Bucolicum carmen*
and many of his other writings".[31] In other words, in the *Rerum vulgarium
fragmenta* the story of the passion for Laura and its poetic re-elaboration
are indistinguishable. The vernacular verses of Petrarch coincide with the
passion which they express. And indeed, according to Benvenuto, the love
sung in the *Fragmenta* is history: it is a direct imprint of lived experience –
it is not poetry.[32]

## Against contingency

It is very likely that Petrarch's reflections on the examples of famous men of
antiquity might encourage a kind of aversion to narrations that do not shun
contemporaneity. On the other hand, it is extremely rare that the present

times are taken by Petrarch as a fount of memorable events: modernity is rather a space emptied of virtue on which the examples produced in happier epochs should be projected. It is known, of course, that there are not lacking excursions into modernity in Petrarch's work. And nevertheless, they do not contradict this portrait. The modern protagonists of the second book of *De vita solitaria* – Celestine V among them – are highly positive examples by virtue of the fact that they have eliminated every contact with their time. Petrarch writes of Celestine that "[he] estimated human things at their true value and trampled beneath his feet the proud head of fortune".[33] So far as the *exempla moderna* gathered in the *Rerum memorandarum libri* are concerned, they are, for the most part, re-adaptations of older narrative forms to new personages.[34] And if we widen our vision to the rest of Petrarch's production, we will perceive that for him the virtues occasionally expressed by the moderns are such only insofar as they conform to ancient virtues. The present time is therefore not the creator of its own virtues: the appreciation of its value is given only when it is possible to find in it a concrete imitation of ancient values ("Stefano Colonna, . . . a man equal to any of the ancients").[35]

The application of ancient narrative and conceptual structures to the modern age seems to be, in effect, the only path available to whomever wishes to describe an epoch about which it would be better to remain silent (*Fam.* VI.4, § 1). From this perspective, it is interesting to read what Petrarch writes in the late *Sen.* XVII.4 in defence of conformity to the truth of the facts narrated in the last novella of the *Decameron*, commonly known as the story of Griselda.[36] Let us read the plot as it is recapitulated in Boccaccio's *rubrica*:

> The Marquis of Saluzzo, overborne by the entreaties of his vassals, consents to take a wife, but, being minded to please himself in the choice of her, takes a husbandman's daughter [Griselda]. He has two children by her, both of whom he makes her believe that he has put to death. Afterward, feigning to be tired of her, and to have taken another wife, he turns her out of doors in her shift, and brings his daughter into the house in guise of his bride; but, finding her patient under it all, he brings her home again, and shews her her children, now grown up, and honours her, and causes her to be honoured, as Marchioness.

For reasons we will shortly examine, Petrarch decides to translate this novella into Latin and to pass it on to his friends. Among the first readers of Petrarch's translation is "a friend . . . from Verona"; this friend, after having read the tale, objects (§§ 6–7): "I believed, and still do, that the whole thing was made up [*ficta omnia credidi et credo*]. For if it were true, what woman anywhere, whether Roman or of any nation whatever will match this Griselda?"[37] Petrarch's reaction is decisive (*Sen.* XVII.4, § 10):

> For who is there . . . who would not think the tales of Curtius and Mucius and the Decii among our people are fictitious, or Codrus and the Philaeni brothers among foreigners, or, since we are speaking of women, Porcia, Hypsicratea, or Alcestis and others like them? And yet the stories are true.

We understand that the precedents cited by Petrarch serve not only to prove the verisimilitude of Boccaccio's story but also to establish its exemplary legitimacy. Petrarch's interlocutor, it will be noted, shares the same system of thought; in his mind, it is not credible that a modern woman should exceed the virtue of ancient women, Roman or foreign as they might have been. Petrarch's reply maintains intact his adversary's criteria of judgement but overturns his conclusions. Precisely by virtue of its consonance with the tales of Curtius and Mucius and the Decii – and above all of Porcia, Hypsicratea, and Alcestis – the story of Griselda, the last of the *Decameron*, is distinguished from all the other novellas of the book (*Sen.* XVII.3, § 7). Thus it befalls that Petrarch, finding himself tormented by grave concerns (§ 8) and finding his mind "torn as usual between various thoughts" (§ 10), discovers that he recognises in Griselda an example wholly equivalent to those of his dear "illustrious ancients".

In the epistle *Sen.* XVII.3, §§ 7–10, we find condensed all the fundamental points of reflection of Petrarch on exemplary literature. Boccaccio's novella has allowed Petrarch to forget the woes that torment him: "it nearly made me forget myself". It has healed, in other words, the passional fracture provoked in Petrarch by his contact with the world, by opposing a universal model of constancy and sufferance of cares provoked by the unstable movement of human things. Insofar as the example of Griselda assumes a universal stature, it must be translated into a language alien to the variability of the vernacular (§ 143): "I decided to retell this story in another language . . . to encourage the readers to imitate . . . this woman's constancy, so that what she maintained toward her husband they may maintain toward our God". In this portrait, the comparison between the tale of Griselda and the ancient examples cited in the following *Sen.* XVII.4 (§ 10) serves to confer to Boccaccio's novella a definitive consecration.

A perfectly identical process is employed, with an assiduity that has no equal in the ancient exegesis of the *Commedia*, by Benvenuto da Imola as well. Indeed, it cannot escape the notice of the reader of Benvenuto's commentary how frequently the modern personages of the poem are set alongside ancient examples – a frequency which cannot help but betray a certain project. A few examples will be sufficient. In the course of Ghibelline convention held in Empoli in 1260, Farinata degli Uberti drew his sword against those who proposed to destroy Florence, and in so doing – writes Benvenuto – "he followed the example of Scipio Africanus, who, at Cannae, after having learned of the slaughter of the Romans, drew his sword against some noblemen who had decided to abandon the fatherland". The innocent Pier della Vigna was forced to commit suicide by Frederick II, just as the innocent "Seneca . . . was constrained to kill himself on account of the cruelty of Nero". King Manfred, cited by Dante in canto III of the *Purgatorio*, "can be described with the words that Livy used to describe Hannibal: 'The great vices of this man equalled his great virtues'". In order to maintain her virginity after her forced departure from a convent, Piccarda Donati (*Par.* III.34–108) "did what had already been done by a young Etruscan of the name Spurinna, who, since his beauty attracted the wives of many men, voluntarily disfigured his face"; and so forth.[38]

## The *Decameron* in the *Commedia*

Even the characters of the *Decameron*, evoked on several occasions in Benvenuto's commentary, are treated in the same way. The uncontrollable rage of Filippo Argenti against Biondello (*Dec.* IX.8) is likened to the brutal sadism of Nero (*ad Inf.* VIII 41–42).[39] The fatal destiny of the murderers of Ghino di Tacco (*Dec.* X.2) is set side by side with that of Caesar's assassins, and Ghino himself is compared first to the centurion Cesius Scaeva and the consul Papirius Cursor, and then to Mucius Scaevola (*ad Purg.* VI.13–14).[40]

Also evident is the commitment with which Benvenuto attempts to reduce not only any rootedness in the present but also the occasional ambiguity of Boccaccio's novellas; and it is evident that the two operations proceed in the same direction. The tales of Ciappelletto, and of Abraham and of Jehannot de Chevigny (*Dec.* I.1–2), are used by Benvenuto as two clear examples 'of faith'. The first serves to illustrate first the rule whereby penitential rites must be founded on an authentic feeling of contrition (*ad Purg.* IX.87) and then the inscrutability of divine judgement (*ad Par.* XX.76–72). The second serves instead to confirm the substantial 'invulnerability' of the Christian faith (*ad Inf.* II.88–93). In both cases the conflictual implications of Boccaccio's narration are deliberately removed.[41] Nothing survives of the ironic tones of the narrator Neifile (§3), in Benvenuto's translation of *Dec.* I.2:

> Pamfilo has shewn by his story that the goodness of God spares to regard our errors when they result from unavoidable ignorance; and in mine I mean to shew you how the same goodness, bearing patiently with the shortcomings of those who should be its faithful witness in

deed and word, draws from them contrariwise evidence of His infallible truth; to the end that what we believe we may with more assured
conviction follow.

Neifile's sarcasm appears clearly once the reader learns the paradoxical
nature of the "evidence of [God's] infallible truth" announced at the opening of the tale (§§ 24–27). Nor are there missing, in the central part of the
novel, moments in which the ancient *exemplum* from which Boccaccio's
invention takes its bearings became the object of explicit parody. Benvenuto's commentary neutralises this tension: "as experiences teach, the holy
word of God cannot be impeded, not by the malice of heretics, nor by the
subtleties of the philosophers, nor by the power of the proud".[42] At the same
time, the disturbing story of Ciappelletto, a character who is almost heroic
in his superhuman dedication to evil (*Dec.* I.1 §§ 10–14), is reduced in
Benvenuto's commentary to a clear *exemplum* about the trivial search for a
"good reputation" (*ad Purg.* IX.87):

> *Beware lest coming up be harmful to you*: [the guardian angel of Purga-
> tory] speaks in a wholly appropriate way, since each day many come to the
> priest to confess, but in reality they mock both him and God. And they act
> in this way so as to seem good men or to leave a good reputation of them-
> selves, as did, for sport, 'Saint Ciappelletto', whose story is narrated beau-
> tifully by Boccaccio di Certaldo, that quietest and most lovable of men.[43]

In the reinterpretation of Benvenuto, the 'particular cases' created by Boccaccio are forcedly represented as 'typical cases'.[44] The true quality of the narrative universe of the *Decameron*, the relentless sense of the mutability of
worldly things,[45] is thus lost: the weft of the plot is simplified, the roles of
the characters are stabilised, the meticulous description of the historical context fades in favour of the immediate revelation of a meaning about which
no doubts can be harboured. It is easy to recognise the affinity between this
use of Boccaccio's book and Petrarch's version of *Griselda*. In that case as
well the final sense of the novella, which Boccaccio himself wisely left sus-
pended,[46] was transformed into a universal teaching (*Sen.* XVII.3, § 143).
The consequences of this process appear clear: though Benvenuto considers
Boccaccio "an attentive investigator of all charming stories", as we have
observed in the previous chapter, he submits Boccaccio's narrative work
to a radical conceptual resizing – almost to an impoverishment. Benvenuto
prefers Boccaccio to Petrarch: but Benvenuto's Boccaccio is an author who
has been thoroughly 'tamed' by Petrarch.

Benvenuto is not the only Dante commentator from the end of the
fourteenth century to use the *Decameron* as a source for interpreting the

*Commedia*. The Anonimo Fiorentino also occasionally inserts some novellas of Boccaccio into his commentary.[47] This should not surprise us. Indeed, it is not rare that Boccaccio chooses characters from Dante's *Commedia* as the protagonists of his tales: for those who, like Benvenuto and the Anonimo Fiorentino, knew both the *Commedia* and the *Decameron*, it was quite natural to compare the one work with the other, whenever Dante's poem offers occasion for it. But the Anonimo Fiorentino uses the *Decameron* in a different way as compared to Benvenuto.

A single example will suffice. The "good Lizio" from Valbona, mentioned in canto XIV of the *Purgatorio* (v. 97), is the protagonist of the (rather licentious) story of Ricciardo Manardi and Caterina (*Dec.* V.4). Let us read the *rubrica*: "Ricciardo Manardi is found by Messer Lizio da Valbona with his daughter, whom he marries, and remains at peace with her father". The words of the rubric are deliberately reticent. In truth, Lizio catches "Ricciardo asleep with her [i.e. Caterina] and in her embrace as described, both being quite naked and uncovered"; and the "embrace" which has already been "described" is the following: "they fell asleep, Caterina's right arm encircling Ricciardo's neck, while with her left hand she held him by that part of his person which your modesty, my ladies, is most averse to name in the company of men".

Predictably, Benvenuto excluded this sentence. He limits himself to remarking that Lizio, when he discovered Caterina with Ricciardo in each other's arms, "prudently and with discretion impelled them to marry, to avoid the compromise of their honour". But Benvenuto does not limit himself to excising: he adds other details, absent in Boccaccio's novella, so as render the figure of Lizio the nobler. Benvenuto writes that Lizio had a son who died prematurely. Since this son was deprived of intelligence ("imbecillis"), and so similar to the dead already before passing away, when Lizio learned of his death he remained unmoved, saying: "It is not news to me that he is dead: he was always like the dead. Just tell me where he has been buried".[48] For his part, the Anonimo Fiorentino reproduces Boccaccio's novella as it is. He summarises it, naturally, but without eliminating any of the most typically 'Boccaccian' details; and above all he does not so much as mention the story of Lizio's "imbecillis" son. The licentious closing line of Lizio is reported by the Anonimo Fiorentino with utmost fidelity: he writes that Lizio "chiamò la moglie et disse: 'Su, madonna Giacomina, vieni a vedere la figliuola tua ch'è tanto stata vaga dell'usignolo ch'ella l'ha preso, et tiellosi in mano'".[49] I here transcribe Boccaccio's version, which in this context serves to offer the reader a faithful English translation of the passage just quoted from the Anonimo Fiorentino's commentary: "Up, up, wife, come and see; for thy daughter has fancied the nightingale to such purpose that she has caught him, and holds him in her hand". The fidelity of the Anonimo Fiorentino to Boccaccio, as can be seen, is total. But in this loyalty we should not recognise a voluntary adhesion to the representation of earthly life in the *Decameron*, or a rejection of the revision of the same effected by Benvenuto. We should rather perceive in it another proof of the substantial passivity with which the Anonimo Fiorentino treated his sources.

## The final confrontation with Petrarch

It would be well now, in closing, to reread the comment on Guido da Montelfeltro by Benvenuto, where we began. I transcribe the passage entire, including the answer that Benvenuto gives to the question put by the mysterious "homines" who criticise Dante for trying to give poetic dignity to modern history:

> I believe . . . that this man [i.e. Guido da Montefeltro] wished to say, quietly, 'Though I do not belong to that happy time in which you, Virgil, and the other great poets have given eternal fame to illustrious men, I deserve nonetheless some sort of fame, or at least I deserve my deeds to be recounted', and in this way he tried to obtain Virgil's good will, as he demonstrated himself worthy of inclusion in a work of poetry. After all, I have no doubt about the fact the Ulysses is more famous [than Guido da Montefeltro], since great poets have written about him: Homer wrote of him in Greek, Virgil in Latin. In the oration that Cicero composed for the poet Archias, he tells us that Alexander the Great, standing in front of the tomb of Achilles, exclaimed: 'O fortunate youth, who was celebrated by so great a singer!', by whom he meant the poet Homer. And it is as if Alexander wished to say: 'I would there were another Homer to tell of my deeds, granting me eternal fame, as happened to Achilles'. Guido da Montefeltro expresses the same concept. But Guido certainly found an excellent poet, even better than what he deserved: namely, Dante. . . . Every day I find men saying: 'What was Dante's aim when he mentions this modern man or this modern episode? He would have done better to write about the illustrious men of ancient times!'. But they often do not know what they are saying, because authors frequently raise and exalt common events and people in their works. I am sure that King Latinus, as well as Turnus or Mezentius, exalted by Virgil (and I do not mention other secondary characters of his poem), were not more important in their historical context than Count Guido da Montefeltro, Malatesta, Maghinardo, and the various other men from Romagna who will be described in this canto.[50]

Benvenuto observes that the nostalgia for an irredeemably passed great-ness, which becomes elusive the more that it is idealised, recurs throughout the history of human thought: this is why Alexander the Great lamented that he had no Homer at hand to sing his deeds. Reread in the light of what we have so far observed, Benvenuto's use of the example of the Macedonian tends to take on a weighty meaning: it seems to suggest that an excess of veneration for the ancient poets can prevent us from recognising the greatness of contemporary ones. And in all probability it is not an accidental fact that Benvenuto employs an oration by Cicero which had been rediscovered by Petrarch[51] to disarm a critique of Dante's poetry which may well have been inspired by Petrarch himself. In the context of Benvenuto's commentary, Alexander the Great's words sound indeed as a warning against the myopia of those who believe that the continuity standing between historical greatness and poetic excellence which characterised ancient times is by now lost and unrepeatable.

The oration *For the poet Archias* offers other noteworthy ideas regarding the problem that interests us here. Cicero confirms that, without the voice of the poets, many exemplary events would remain buried beneath the dark-ness of history (§14). As regards the quest for fame and virtue, we read,

> all literature, all philosophy, all history, abounds with incentives to noble actions, incentives which would be buried in black darkness were the light of the written word not flashed upon them. How many pictures of high endeavour the great authors of Greece and Rome have drawn for our use, and bequeathed to us, not only for our contemplation, but for our emulation.

The expression "which would be buried in black darkness were the light of the written word not flashed upon them" can be set side by side with a formula used by Benvenuto in his comment on *Inf.* XX.1–3: Benvenuto writes that Dante, first and foremost, "brought back to the light" historical figures in whom nobody had ever been interested.[52] Benvenuto is referring evidently to the contemporary characters of the *Commedia*, who had before then been known less to the poets than to the chroniclers. It might be use-ful to compare these words to another passage from Benvenuto's oeuvre, contained in the comment on Lucan's *Pharsalia*:

> All . . . the commentators say that Lucan is so called because was the 'singer of light', meaning that he brought a history which had been bur-ied in the darkness back to the light; but this is false. In fact, Titus Livy described this same history in prose, with a clear and extremely elegant style; similarly, Julius Celsus, who accompanied Caesar in many of

his most important deeds, describes the same events with exceptional clarity. I would rather say then that Lucan narrated, in an obscure and artificial way, a history that had already been narrated in a perfectly limpid way.[53]

Lucan, in other words, did precisely the contrary of Dante: he made "obscure" – which is to say, difficult to understand – the memory of facts and characters of which other writers had already spoken clearly. Why is this comparison between Lucan and Dante of interest? Because it gives us to understand that, in Benvenuto's eyes, whoever reproduces already famous stories does not do any great service to his readers – above all if he tells those stories employing excessive rhetorical artifices, rendering the understanding of the text unnecessarily complicated. But who, in the years surrounding Benvenuto's activity, had undertaken an operation quite similar to Lucan's? Petrarch, naturally. We do not know what Benvenuto thought of Petrarch's *Africa*; indeed, it is not even sure that he read it.[54] Nevertheless it does not escape Benvenuto's notice that similarities exist between the *Africa* and the *Pharsalia*: "Lucan entitled his poem *Pharsalia* because the story that he tells takes place in Pharsalus; similarly, Petrarch's poem is entitled *Africa* because is it about the wars that were fought in Africa".[55] Are we to conclude therefore that, according to Benvenuto, Petrarch, like Lucan, has obscured historical events which others had narrated limpidly? Benvenuto never says as much. On the other hand, the most famous opponent of the *Tre Corone*, Niccolò Niccoli, does say it, and entirely explicitly (*Dialogi ad Petrum Paulum Histrum* I, § 48): "Look how great is the difference between this poet [i.e. Petrarch] and our Virgil. Virgil with his poem made obscure men illustrious with his poetry, while Petrarch did all he could to make a very famous man, Scipio Africanus, obscure".[56]

Let us return to Cicero's *For the poet Archias*. In the passage that I have transcribed above (§ 14), Cicero seems to reaffirm the unconditional cult for ancient examples ("exemplorum vetustas") and for writers of the past. But this is not quite true. At the point where he describes the qualities of the poet Archias, Cicero indeed tells (§ 18): "how often . . . have I seen him . . . extemporizing quantities of excellent verse dealing with current topics!" Thus we learn that Archias in no way despises contemporary subjects ("current topics", "quae tum agerentur"). As a good poet, Archias aims instead to enhance these through his style, and in this way he sets himself on the path set by the great writers of the past: "To his finished and studied work I have known such approval accorded that his glory rivalled that of the great writers of antiquity".

Similarly, Benvenuto's Dante does not give new life to the classics by limiting himself to repeating their contents, but rather he has assimilated the lesson of the classics to such an extent that he is able to apply it as much to his own times as to the entire course of human events, in this way liberating the ethical and cognitive potential of each story. In the face of this, it is senseless to ask why Dante mentioned Guido da Montefeltro in the *Commedia* whilst keeping silent about an important Virgilian character like Mezentius: both Guido and Mezentius belong to the same dimension – a historical, indeed a transient dimension – from which it follows that between their lives no substantial qualitative difference is to be found. To neglect all of this is equivalent to failing to understand the role of poetry in the elaboration of the collective memory. The recognition of the constants that orient the movements of human history depends essentially on the gaze that literature casts upon the world. For this reason too, the merit of knowing how to describe and 'magnify' the line separating the universal from the particular, the eternally valid example from pure contingency, must be attributed to the poets more than to anyone else.

## Notes

1 See L. Fiorentini, *Per Benvenuto da Imola* (Bologna: il Mulino, 2016), 90–99.
2 See L. Fiorentini, 'Portraits d'Averroès et de ses (prétendus) adeptes dans les anciens commentaires sur la *Comédie*', in *Dante et l'averroïsme*, ed. by A. de Libera, J.-B. Brenet and I. Rosier-Catach (Paris: Collège de France-Les Belles Lettres, 2019), 201–208.
3 See Fiorentini, *Per Benvenuto da Imola*, 95–99 and 143–146. See also L. Fiorentini, 'Spiegare Dante attraverso la storia', in *Intorno a Dante*, ed. by L. Azzetta and A. Mazzucchi (Rome: Salerno, 2018), 439–444, and 'I regni danteschi come allegorie della vita civile e dei suoi limiti. Su alcune implicazioni politiche della prima ricezione della *Commedia*', *Philosophical Readings* 12/1 (2020), 183–195.
4 Benvenuto da Imola, *Comentum super Dantis Aldigherij "Comoediam"*, ed. by G. F. Lacaita, 5 tomes (Florence: Barbera, 1887), tome 2, 300. For an initial, partial analysis of this passage, see L. Fiorentini, 'Archaeology of the *Tre Corone*', *Dante Studies* 136 (2018), 13–17.
5 *The Divine Comedy of Dante Alighieri*, I, *Inferno*, ed. and trans. by R. M. Durling, introduction and notes by R. L. Martinez and R. M. Durling (New York-Oxford: Oxford University Press, 1996).
6 Benvenuto da Imola, *Comentum*, tome 2, 299–300.
7 See the manuscript Ashburnham 839, f. 60*r-v*: "credo quod Guido fuerit homo valentior quam fuerit unquam Ulixes. Ideo Dantes hoc dicit, quasi dicat: 'Feci tanta quod unusquis[que] bene potuisset describere de factis meis'".
8 Benvenuto da Imola, *Comentum*, tome 2, 300.
9 I quote the translation by N. H. Watts: see Cicero, *The Speeches (Pro Archia poeta, Post reditum in senatu, Post reditum ad Quirites, De domo sua, De*

*haruspicum responsis, Pro Plancio)*, trans. by N. H. Watts (London-New York: W. Heinemann-G. P. Putnam's Sons, 1923).

10  See Fiorentini, *Per Benvenuto da Imola*, 288–296.

11  See L. C. Rossi, *Studi su Benvenuto da Imola* (Florence: Sismel Edizioni del Galluzzo, 2016), 166–180.

12  Translation is mine. See C. Salutati, *Epistolario*, ed by F. Novati, 4 vols. (Rome: Istituto storico italiano, 1891–1911), vol. 3 (1893), 373. On this passage, see S. Gilson, *Dante and Renaissance Florence* (Cambridge: Cambridge University Press, 2005), 61–63.

13  I have spoken of the judgement passed by Niccolò Niccoli on Dante, Petrarch and Boccaccio in the *Prologue* of this book. I will shortly return to these passages.

14  See L. Bruni, *Dialogi ad Petrum Paulum Histrum*, ed. by S. U. Baldassarri (Florence: Olschki, 1994), 267. Translation mine. On the *Dialogi* by Leonardo Bruni, see H. Baron, *The Crisis of the Early Italian Renaissance: Civic Humanism and Republican Liberty in an Age of Classicism and Tyranny*, 2 vols. (Princeton, NJ: Princeton University Press, 1955), vol. 1, 190–245, and Gilson, *Dante and Renaissance Florence*, 83–96.

15  L. Bruni, *Le vite di Dante e del Petrarca*, ed. by M. Berté and R. Rognoni, in *Le vite di Dante dal XIV al XVI secolo*, ed. by M. Berté, M. Fiorilla, S. Chiodo and I. Valente (Rome: Salerno, 2017), 245.

16  See Gilson, *Dante and Renaissance Florence*, 78–83.

17  See A. Lanza, *Polemiche e berte letterarie nella Firenze del primo Quattrocento* (Rome: Bulzoni, 1971), 98. Translation mine.

18  See Lanza, *Polemiche e berte letterarie*, 263–264.

19  See Bruni, *Le vite di Dante e del Petrarca*, 244.

20  Bruni, *Dialogi*, 255–256.

21  See Lanza, *Polemiche e berte letterarie*, 264.

22  Here and in what follows, I employ the 'classic' translation of J. M. Rigg: see *The "Decameron" of Giovanni Boccaccio*, faithfully trans. by J. M. Rigg (London: Routledge, 1921).

23  In this chapter too I quote from the translation of Aldo S. Bernardo: see F. Petrarch, *Letters on Familiar Matters, Rerum familiarum libri I–VIII*, trans. by A. S. Bernardo (New York: Italica Press, 2005), 314–317.

24  C. Delcorno, *"Exemplum" e letteratura tra Medioevo e Rinascimento* (Bologna: il Mulino, 1989), 231. Translation mine.

25  See E. Fenzi, 'Petrarca e l'esilio: uno stile di vita', *Arzanà* 16–17 (2013), 396–399.

26  Fenzi, 'Petrarca e l'esilio', 97. Translation mine.

27  See F. Petrarca, *Invectives*, ed. and trans. by D. Marsh (Cambridge, MA-London, England: The I Tatti Renaissance Library-Harvard University Press, 2003).

28  I quote the draft 'γ' of the letter, which corresponds to the text which was sent to Benvenuto: see Rossi, *Studi su Benvenuto da Imola*, 200–202 (translation mine).

29  In this chapter too I quote from the translation of the *Seniles* by Aldo S. Bernardo: see here F. Petrarch, *Letters of Old Age: Rerum senilium libri I–XVIII*, vol. 2, *Books X–XVIII*, tranl. by A. S. Bernardo, S. Levin and R. A. Bernardo (New York: Italica Press, 2005), 588–589.

30  Benvenuto da Imola, *Comentum*, tome 4, 75 (*ad Purg*. XXIV.52–54).

31  Benvenuto da Imola, *Comentum*, tome 1, 83 (*ad Inf*. II.52–54). See previous chapter.

32  For a broader view of the question, see S. Gentili, 'Poesia e immagine: storia di un'idea da Boezio a Boccaccio', *Letteratura e arte* 16 (2018), 159–174.

33  See F. Petrarch, *The Life of Solitude*, trans. by J. Zeitlin (Urbana, IL: University of Illinois Press, 1924).

34  See Delcorno, *"Exemplum" e letteratura*, 235.

35  This passage has been drawn from the epistle *To Posterity*, § 17. I quote the translation of Karl Enenkel: see *Modelling the Individual: Biography and Portrait in the Renaissance*, ed. by K. Enenkel, B. de Jong-Crane and P. Liebregts (Amsterdam-Atlanta: Rodopi, 1998), 257–281. See also the essay by Enenkel contained in the same volume: 'Modelling the Humanist: Petrarch's Letter *To Posterity* and Boccaccio's Biography of the Poet Laureate', 11–49.

36  On the translation of *Griselda* made by Petrarch, see D. Wallace, 'Letters of Old Age: Love between Men, Griselda, and Farewell to Letters', in *Petrarch: A Critical Guide to the Complete Works*, ed. by V. Kirkham and A. Maggi (Chicago: Chicago University Press, 2009), 321–330.

37  The translation in this case too is by Aldo S. Bernardo: see Petrarch, *Letters of Old Age: Rerum senilium libri I-XVIII*, vol. 2, *Books X–XVIII*, 669–671.

38  The cited passages are taken from Benvenuto da Imola, *Comentum*: see, respectively, tome 1, 349–350 (Farinata); tome 1, 440–441 (Pier della Vigna); tome 3, 102 (Manfred); tome 4, 367 (Piccarda). For further examples and analysis, I refer the reader to Fiorentini, *Per Benvenuto da Imola*, 331–364.

39  See Benvenuto da Imola, *Comentum*, tome 1, 284–287, and Fiorentini, *Per Benvenuto da Imola*, 495–501.

40  See Benvenuto da Imola, *Comentum*, tome 3, 169–171.

41  For a general overview on this point, see the illuminating study by K. Flasch, *Giovanni Boccaccio. Poesie nach de Pest. De Anfang des "Decameron"* (Mainz: Dieterich'sche Verlagsbuchhandlung, 1992). See also M. Lavagetto, *Oltre le usate leggi. Una lettura del "Decameron"* (Turin: Einaudi, 2019), 133–143.

42  Benvenuto da Imola, *Comentum*, tome 1, 95.

43  Benvenuto da Imola, *Comentum*, tome 3, 264–265.

44  See H.-J. Neuschäfer, *Boccaccio un der Beginn der Novelle* (Munich: Fink, 1969), 33–43.

45  For a general overview of this question, see T. Barolini, 'The Wheel of the *Decameron*', *Romance Philology* 36/4 (1983), 521–539.

46  The narrator of the novella, Dioneo, praises Griselda, but, in contrast to Petrarch, gives the reader to understand that her model of comportment *should not* be followed (§§ 68–69). See T. Barolini, 'The Marquis of Saluzzo, or the Griselda Story before It Was Hijacked: Calculating Matrimonial Odds in *Decameron* X.10', *Mediaevalia* 34 (2013), 23–55.

47  See F. Rocco, 'Presenze boccacciane nel commento dantesco dell'Anonimo Fiorentino', *Studi sul Boccaccio* 11 (1979), 409–410.

48  Benvenuto da Imola, *Comentum*, tome 3, 388–389.

49  *Commento alla "Divina Commedia" d'Anonimo Fiorentino del secolo XIV*, ed. by P. Fanfani, 3 tomes (Bologna: Romagnoli, 1866–1874), tome 2, 228.

50  Benvenuto da Imola, *Comentum*, tome 2, 300.

51  On Petrarch's discovery of the oration *For the poet Archias*, see M. Berté, 'Petrarca, Salutati e le orazioni di Cicerone', in *Manoscritti e lettori di Cicerone tra Medioevo e Umanesimo*, ed. by P. De Paolis (Cassino: Università degli Studi di Cassino e del Lazio Meridionale, 2012), 21–52 (with its wide bibliography).

52  Benvenuto da Imola, *Comentum*, tome 2, 64.

53  For the original version of this passage, see Rossi, *Studi su Benvenuto da Imola*, 37–38. Translation is mine.

54  See Rossi, *Studi su Benvenuto da Imola*, 154–155.

55  See again Rossi, *Studi su Benvenuto da Imola*, 42–43.

56  Bruni, *Dialogi*, 257.

# Epilogue

The friar Ilaro, in his (by now) famous letter transmitted to us by Boccaccio, reports that Dante chose to write the *Commedia* in the vernacular because he was forced to do so by the decadence of the times. Dante had noticed that the liberal arts had definitively faded, or, to state things more precisely, that they had become the domain of the uncultivated ("And so men of high birth, for whom such works were written in a better age have – shame on them! – abandoned the liberal arts to the common folk").[1] As we have seen in the last chapter, Benvenuto da Imola emphatically denies that this is the case. In fact, in his opinion, precisely the contrary is true: only one blinded by excessive – and in the final analysis irrational – nostalgia for the past could share the idea expressed by the 'Dante' of Ilaro's epistle.

It is possible that in the words of Ilaro's Dante there is hidden some concern, analogous to that expressed by the "homines" who criticise Dante for giving space, in his *Commedia*, to modern events and characters: if one too passively bends to the demands of the present, especially when this present appears to be culturally degraded, one risks bringing about a final oblivion of the illustrious examples of ancient times, transmitted by the great poets of the past. In other words, one risks forcing the glorious Muses of the classics into a final silence. But this concern, too, according to Benvenuto, is senseless. The 'true' Dante had perfect knowledge of the ancient literary tradition; he had assimilated its meaning to such an extent that he could make manifest its universal implications – implications which, being universal, were applicable to every epoch of history. Dante's critics, in other words, did not understand that it is the mechanical repetition of what has already been written which renders the Muses' voices feeble, not the search for new forms of poetical expression. A clear example of this attitude of closure toward the modern poets can be found in the words of Niccolò Niccoli that I quoted in the *Prologue*: "I prefer by far a single letter of Cicero, or a single ode by Virgil, to all the minor works of these authors of yours" (*Dialogi ad Petrum Paulum Histrum* I, § 50).[2]

Boccaccio, too, in his letter of 1371 to Iacopo Pizzinga (*Ep.* XIX), defended a thesis apparently similar to Benvenuto's:

> our Dante Alighieri drew the sweet water from a fount which had been abandoned for many centuries. However, he did not do this by following the same path tread by the ancients, but he chose to follow other paths, not without fatigue. And in this way he came, first of all, to turn his gaze to the sky and to summit the mountain, and he reached the aim that he had set out to reach: to reawaken the sleeping Muses and return to Apollo his cithara.[3]

For Boccaccio, the 'other path' was essentially, as we know, that of the vernacular – with all its attendant problems. For Benvenuto, the 'other path' was another still: it was that which brought Dante to gather together in a single work the historical events of every period, both ancient and modern, and to order them according to a criterion that was at once advantageous from a poetic point of view and effective from a moral one.

According to the interpretation of Benvenuto da Imola, Dante's *Commedia* is a work in which the contingent and mutable are permitted no space. Consequently, the *Commedia* stands at the greatest possible distance from those literary forms that deliberately take as their primary subject the changeability of human things. But what led Benvenuto to this conclusion was not the idea of history elaborated by Dante in the *Commedia* – the conviction, that is, that all human actions are ordered by Providence according to a principle that might be known – but rather the lesson of Petrarch on the function of illustrious examples and on the sense of historical narration.

By this depiction, Boccaccio is cast into a marginal position. He is considered above all as an interpreter of Dante rather than as an author in his own right. Beyond this, his greatest work, the *Decameron*, suffers from marked deformations and considerable conceptual weakening at the hands of its first readers. In the commentary of Benvenuto, above all, the *Decameron* is transformed into a simple collection of exemplary novellas, of tales aimed at giving expression to universal and immutable values, which are therefore alien to the unpredictable forces of reality. But it is evident that Boccaccio, in the *Decameron*, moves in the opposite direction of that delineated by Benvenuto: the specific characteristic of the *Decameron*'s tales is precisely their faithful description of human actions insofar as these are subject to the power of fortune. The line of continuity stretching between Dante, Petrarch and Boccaccio is to be found, according to Benvenuto da Imola, in the exclusion of everything mutable and contingent from the sphere of poetry. But to recognise this line of continuity is to bury the peculiar qualities of Boccaccio's writing, actually annihilating it.

The Anonimo Fiorentino appears, from this point of view, more respectful toward the authentic meaning of the *Decameron*'s narration. But, as we have observed, the Anonimo Fiorentino does not represent a true exception to the rule: his fidelity to the ambiguity in Boccaccio's narration is owed more to the essential passivity with which he treats his sources than to any conscious adhesion to the narrative universe of the *Decameron*.[4]

It might be said therefore that it was Petrarch, in the last analysis, who laid down the law in the oldest phase of the formation of the *Tre Corone* canon. Even those who, like Benvenuto, explicitly reject some of his poetic rules – and above all, his devaluation of the vernacular – cannot help but share the spirit underpinning them: literature must make itself into the vehicle for immutable and universal values, and it must avoid, in consequence, all contact with what is mutable and transient.

However, there is at least a single other criterion which explains the early association of the names of Dante, Petrarch and Boccaccio in commentaries on the *Commedia* – a criterion often perceived even by commentators who, in contrast to Benvenuto, demonstrate a narrower and less thorough knowledge of the works of Petrarch and Boccaccio. What criterion is this? By way of response, we read another passage – the last one – of the invective which Niccolò Niccoli addressed against the *Tre Corone* in the first book of Leonardo Bruni's *Dialogi*. Niccoli says (§ 50):

> They [i.e. Dante, Petrarch and Boccaccio] share a common defect: they were all extremely arrogant, because they believed that no one could judge their works better than they could, and beyond this they held that everyone would express the same esteem for them that they felt for themselves. One of them calls himself *poeta*, the other *laureatus*, the third *vatis*! The wretches; what a mist obscures their gaze![5]

Leaving aside the polemical tone of these words, we see that Niccoli grasps an important element which Dante, Petrarch and Boccaccio held in common: all three of them, beyond composing poetic works, dedicated their energies also toward reasoning on the proper role of poets and on poetry as such. In other words, in the work of the *Tre Corone*, poetic writing and the theory of poetry are inseparable.

The earliest Dante commentators already perceived this fundamental element of continuity between Dante, Petrarch and Boccaccio: and indeed, as we have seen, they cite Petrarch and Boccaccio above all in the context of examining Dante's poetry from a theoretical point of view. It should hardly astound us that it was the ancient interpreters of the *Commedia* to first recognise the continuity between Dante, Petrarch and Boccaccio in their reflections on poetry. From the very first (mythical) reader of the

*Inferno*, the friar Ilaro, all the way up to the most influential scholars of the twentieth century – Croce, Auerbach, Singleton . . . – Dante's *Commedia* is indubitably the first modern text which has encouraged, by its very nature, great reflections of this kind.

## Notes

1 I quote once more from the translation of Philip H. Wicksteed: see G. Boccaccio, *Life of Dante*, trans. by P. H. Wicksteed and ed. by W. Chamberlin (Richmond, UK: Oneworld Classics, 2009), 105–107.
2 L. Bruni, *Dialogi ad Petrum Paulum Histrum*, ed. by S. U. Baldassarri (Florence: Olschki, 1994), 258. Translation is mine.
3 G. Boccaccio, *Tutte le opere*, vol. V/1, ed. by V. Branca *et alii* (Milan: Mondadori, 1992), 666. Translation is mine. On this passage, see M. Eisner, *Boccaccio and the Invention of Italian Literature* (Cambridge: Cambridge University Press, 2013), 24–25.
4 On the reception of Boccaccio in the fifteenth century, see the recent volume *A Boccaccian Renaissance: Essays on the Early Modern Impact of Giovanni Boccaccio and His Works*, ed. by M. Eisner and D. Lummus (Notre Dame, IN: University of Notre Dame Press, 2019).
5 Bruni, *Dialogi*, 258.

# Index

## People's names

Dante, Petrarch and Boccaccio's names are not included, as they are quoted in almost every page of this book. All the mentions of their works are recorded in the 'Literary works' section of the index.

## Literary works

Printed in the United States
by Baker & Taylor Publisher Services